Praise for

Bailing Out the Company Canoe

Become a Better Boss

"*Bailing Out the Company Canoe* would be a joy to read if it weren't so painful. Oh, how it made me look at myself, and all those who think themselves to be entrepreneurs, only to discover that they are actually asleep! Wonderful, wonderful, wonderful read!"
Michael Gerber, bestselling author of *The E Myth* book series

"*Bailing Out the Company Canoe* gives you a rare and unique inside view of a dot-com demise from startup to finish, chronicled by 16 employees who gave it life but were powerless to stop its inept Founder from killing it before it could walk. You'll learn more about management from the personal accounts in *Bailing Out the Company Canoe* than from any academic case-study!"
Marilyn Haight, author of *Who's Afraid of the Big, Bad Boss? 13 Types and How to Survive Them*

"*Bailing Out the Company Canoe* is a must read for every aspiring leader. The saga it describes is riveting and the lessons it provides offer a practical manual for career success and fulfillment."
Michael Feiner author of *The Feiner Points of Leadership: The 50 Basic Laws That Will Make People Want to Perform Better For You*

Bailing Out the Company Canoe

Become a Better Boss

R. H. FRANCK

Written for those who manage people
and written by those who do the work
with the goal of adding common sense to the workplace.

Introduction - A Note from the Contributors

Why Did We Write This Book? We Say We Want an Evolution!
(With an apology to the Beatles)

It is time for a management book written by employees because only employees know that their productivity could easily be increased if the management skills of their bosses could be magically improved. It is time to re-train bosses across the US and upgrade their current management style, which likely mirrors that of their own former ineffective bosses, to a goal-achieving management style that fits the employees. This new style of management is rooted in increasing company revenues and profits through greater employee productivity.

But first, the manager must understand what the employee's job is, how the employees actually do their jobs, and what the employees need to complete tasks with the goal of moving the department, division, and company forward. It is time to replace a management style that reluctantly and distastefully manages employees with a new confident management style that is fueled by a boss who knows what skills the team has and knows how best to get the work done. We are saying "Enough already."

So, who really needs to read this book?

• You do if you are a manager who feels that you are not organizing, staffing, and understanding your employee's skills and you want to become a better boss;

• If you are an employee who aspires to become a manager, this book will show you how to correct common managerial mistakes. Try these new techniques on the small group of employees you currently work with and see if you can improve just your own team. This book is for you if you want to quickly move from Beginning Manager to Star Manager;

• And if you are a Business School faculty member you can use this book to broaden how you teach management skills to your students. So very often business is not about the manager, but it is rather about how the manager transforms innate skills, education, and talents of the managed into great products and services. A central theme of this book is to redirect the spotlight onto the managed and take it away from the manager;

• All graduate school business students should read this book because they have the most immediate opportunity to improve the workplace. Many companies have a "fast track" and these managers who have the advantage of an advanced degree will have the opportunity to apply what they have learned from this book to quickly affect positive change in the workplace;

• All undergraduate business students should read this book because it will take them into a real workplace where they can see and hear what truly goes on, and for which they must be prepared. Business students should discuss this book with people they admire and even with those they don't admire, because the workforce has both these types of employees.

Bailing Out the Company Canoe is the lively story of our business tragedy. We were optimistic when we joined the Company and optimistic when we had early success. We are now optimistic that much can be learned from our experiences and observations. We followed the Founder as well as the Chairman for far too long because we believed in our revolutionary products and in the judgment of our industry-leading customers. Now we want other employees to benefit from what we learned and to judge correctly whom they should follow. We want our readers to understand why they should follow any particular business leader and, most importantly, when they should stop following.

Our Acronym Guide

ASVP: Acquired Senior Vice President

CEO: Chief Executive Officer

CFO: Chief Financial Officers 1, 2, and 3

COO1, 2, 3: Chief Operating Officers 1, 2, and 3

CSR: Customer Service Representative

CTO1, 2, 3: Chief Technology Officers 1, 2, and 3

DQD: Director of Quantitative Data

EVP: Executive Vice President, Sales and Marketing

FCC: Final Consultant to the Company

FEA: The Founder's Final Executive Assistant

HoS: Head of Sales

HR: Human Resources

IBM: Investor and Board Member

IT Department: Information Technology Department

PTB: Part Time Bookkeeper

SOM: Saintly Office Manager

VC: Venture Capitalist

VP: Vice President

Chapter 1: Lessons from Losing

Contributor: The Vice President (VP)

Narrator: The Vice President (VP) experienced the lifecycle of the Company, from start-up to shut down. She was one of three senior managers in the earliest days of the Company when there were fewer than twenty employees. She was hired to represent the business, rather than the technology, side of developing the web-based products. After the successful launch of the web products she stayed with the Company until the end, because of her complete belief in the products she was instrumental in creating. What follows are the business practices that the VP believes contributed to the failure of the Company.

In the past five years it has not been unusual when a Company with a team of bright, hard-working, attractive, competitive, resourceful, talented, witty employees fails. And ours did. But the failure was not due to financial skullduggery; our finances were complicated, but not furtive or even very interesting. It was not due to middle mis-management; the middle managers bravely bailed the canoe out every morning and kept much of the real work of the Company on track. Product obsolescence can't be blamed; our products woke up a sleepy industry and our customers called them "addictive."   Nor can bloated payrolls be the cause; we often went without pay, took stock instead of pay, or went on 50% pay to get over the next rough patch. Despite these efforts, our Company failed for far more deadly reasons.

How could we fail?   We were seasoned, talented professionals. We developed a first-of-its-kind product that solved an industry problem. We had the best customers in our industry and they loved our products. Why did we fail??

I would like to introduce myself. I am the Vice President (VP) responsible for taking the original vision of the Founder of our Company and developing it, with our software engineers, into a web-based suite of products. I was with the Company for a little over five years and witnessed its entire lifecycle, from high energy start-up, to mid-life stall, and then the painfully slow demise. The failure of the Company was the first professional failure of my 31-year career and it took me by surprise because I believed, until I joined the Company, that hard work, a great product, and persistence would result in professional success.

At the time of the founding of our Company, professionals in our industry made a routine but high-risk decision that historically had a 40% failure rate. They typically made this business decision by combining professional intuition with a research process that involved extracting precise data from six separate databases. This research process was costly, cumbersome, labor intensive, and required from eight to twelve working days to accomplish, depending on the experience of the assisting staff person. The end result of this critical analysis was a sales and revenue projection that would mean profits only if the projection was correct. The projection was then included in a final report for executive committee review and decision. Keep in mind that these costly, critical decisions were wrong 40% of the time.

The Founder of our Company had a brilliant vision and proposed developing a product that would revolutionize the way our industry made this critical decision and improve its success rate. The goal was to automate, shorten and simplify the research process by making key data instantly available via the Internet rather than by mail or fax. We wanted to improve the accuracy of our industry's critical decision by providing pertinent data. We also envisioned developing a rating system to give our customers a frame of reference in which to make this expensive decision. These were the initial goals of our start-up Company.

Early on, we licensed appropriate data and integrated them into a single database to quickly and easily generate reports that looked like the ones that were placed in those executive committee reports. We also, as our Chief Scientist loved to say, "added intelligence to data" by incorporating the Founder's envisioned index to give our clients a way of gauging how successful the market they were researching might be for their company. This, in effect, reduced the "intuition" in the process and replaced it with a bit of science.

We were successful in making our products available to our clients over the Internet. This major accomplishment set us apart from our faxing-and-express-mailing competitors and took the eight to twelve-day ordeal and turned it into a ten second on-line experience. For an annual subscription fee, our customers could access this essential data as frequently as necessary. The data our industry prized became instantly accessible, affordable, and available on an unlimited basis to anyone in our client's company with a password to our web site. In addition, our web-based products were so easy to use that we often trained our client's summer help how to use them.

We then expanded on the original vision of the Founder. We successfully added new web-based products to our site that enabled our clients to define clearly and specifically who their customers were and identify where those customers lived in a proposed new market. Our system counted those prospective customers and helped our clients judge instantly if there were a sufficient number of their potential customers in the new market to support their business. Additionally, our clients could use our products to find and advertise to their potential customers in existing but underperforming markets. This resulted in improved business performance and our savvy clients were thrilled.

Several miracles occurred. First, our products worked so well that the historic 40% failure rate associated with this day-in-and-day-out decision making process dropped dramatically and saved our clients millions of dollars. Second, we convinced a technophobic industry to try a little technology and many clients became, in their words, "hooked" on our products. Third, our client roster grew to include the most innovative, prestigious and fastest growing companies in our industry. How could this initially successful, promising Company have spun so completely out of control?

A series of top-level hiring mistakes were made that crippled the ability of our Company to make effective decisions. For example, the new Chairman, who was from an unrelated industry, stopped the development of our incomplete web-based products leaving us with only part of our original story to sell. Then he and the Founder decided that generating investment dollars rather than sales revenue was to become their priority. This decision left us incapable of becoming self-sustaining. In a subsequent, desperate attempt to stabilize our revenue stream, the Founder and the Chairman acquired two complementary firms. They killed the revenue stream of the first, viable thirty-five-year-old firm within two years. The second firm turned out to have no revenue prospects after the merger was completed.

Then disaster seeped into our Company when every mistake that first-time managers typically make was made enthusiastically by the Founder and the Chairman.

First, the Founder and the Chairman had no understanding of how to price and sell an innovative product. They could not and would not develop a focused marketing plan to get us from our early, inquisitive, adventurous, customers to the mainstream customers. Second, the Founder, an inexperienced manager, was incapable of personal assessment and refused to consider hiring someone who could help us realize the dream. Third, no one at the senior management level was held accountable for their decisions. The lack of a review process resulted in bad decisions spawning even worse decisions. To those serious problems add:

- Poor internal communication,
- Antagonistic relationships with crucial vendors,
- Useless employees who were elevated to Sacred Cow status by the Founder,
- A remote office in each US time zone,
- Senior decision-makers with no industry experience.

It is hard to believe that our Company lasted five minutes let alone five years. However, the collective will of the employees was strong, and the collective strength of the job market at the time was weak.

The lessons I learned working with the Company were professionally and personally gigantic. Let me start with these:

- Scrutinize whom you are following. The vision of the Founder/Chairman/boss you are following may be great, but how is the vision being developed, managed and marketed?

- Examine why you are following. Whose dream are you chasing – yours, or that of your Founder/Chairman/boss? You may be able to trick yourself into believing that you are following your dream but one Sunday afternoon ask yourself out loud what was accomplished at work in the past month. Now listen to yourself answer this question. If the accomplishments you can list out loud were on your agenda for the Company, that is great and you have nothing much to be concerned about. If the accomplishments were not on your agenda but on the agenda of the Founder/Chairman/boss and make no sense to you, you may be in trouble and you need to face this.

- How long are you planning on following your Founder/Chairman/boss? The most important word in that sentence is "planning." You must decide how long you are going to follow and then stick to it. You cannot go in day after day trying to do your best work yet go home night after night thwarted. This guarantees that you will have high blood pressure, a condition so boring that everyone assumes it is a self-inflicted wound. And it is. Set a date and if there is no progress on your agenda even though you are working hard, move on.

Chapter 2: In the Beginning

Contributor: Jill-of-all-Trades, the Fifth Employee

> **Narrator:** *We start with the observations of the Jill-of-all-Trades who was a resourceful and talented employee. Jill installed and taught herself a score of complex software programs to produce reports and custom maps that rivaled those generated by major consulting firms. Jill was a gifted employee who was always pushing herself to learn and produce more for the Company. She grew from receptionist to advanced mapping specialist in less than a year and was our secret weapon on many custom assignments.*

Oh, no. The marijuana smells really strong on his clothes today. He will now hover, unfocused, in my cubicle until I want to slap him. How can the Founder be so gullible as to think this guy is useful? He knows nothing, he does nothing, and he has vague, strange opinions on everything related to technology because he cannot think linearly. How can I put him into perspective for you? There is a character in the cartoon strip *Zits,* named Jeremy. This guy has the same dark t-shirt as Jeremy, a wardrobe of similar plaid flannel shirts, the same loose pants and huge shoes, the identical van, and floppy hair. Except Jeremy is fifteen years old and this fellow is thirty-seven.

The Founder thinks he is great, and that our Company would fold without him to oversee our technology, never mind that I installed all of the software and taught myself how to use it so that we, a shop of five people, were able to produce custom maps and good-looking reports. Could it be that the Founder just can't see that he is a mistake and wastes our valuable resources, such as time, money, and energy? (One of the people in our office is a NASA/space nut. He nicknamed him Project Mercury, which you may remember was the US effort back in the 60s to see if man could live in space. Boy, could we have saved NASA a ton of money.) But maybe the Founder just can't admit to making a mistake when Project Mercury was hired? He drives me crazy.

I came on board because the Founder told me I was joining a fast-paced, technology based, start-up Company, and that my low salary would be supplemented by stock options that I hoped would be worth a good amount of money in the future. My job interview with the Founder was at a great Italian restaurant. I was asked a couple of questions about my background and skills, and as the martinis the Founder ordered arrived, the Founder launched into the tale of starting the Company. The idea for the Company was developed while the Founder was on vacation at a deluxe golf course in Arizona. The theory was that it was possible to combine several databases and produce a web-based product with the goal that it would become the industry standard, or something like that. Who knew if this was possible? But the office was about fourteen minutes from my house, I could wear jeans to work, the martini kicked in, and so I said yes.

In the beginning there were five of us. The Founder; Project Mercury, (Director of Research was his title no less; what a joke); a Part-Time Bookkeeper; and a funny, kind, ex-real estate broker (Senior Associate) looking for a windfall. That was the group I joined.

The Company was housed in a very small space in a nice suburban office park. We barely fit into the space ourselves, and then the Founder hired a team of eight consulting software engineers. The team consisted of their Project Manager, a Senior Engineer, and six additional junior engineers. They arrived early one Monday morning to begin work. I was there by myself, of course. The Founder was working out with a personal physical trainer. Project Mercury didn't usually arrive until around 10:30am, and the Part-Time Bookkeeper (PTB) was at her soy-organic kale-peace meditation class. What was I to do with all of these consultants?

The Founder had not bothered to mention to me when they were to arrive. Well, we had a seldom-used conference room, so I thought they would just have to share it. I began plugging in all of their computers and hauled a small desk into a corner of the room, so their Project Manager could have the pretense of a desk and his own space. Our funny, kind, Senior Associate arrived, and he helped me plug things in and move and hook up phones, which I showed the consultants how to use. I gave them the restroom tour, and told them how to use the microwave, which was balanced on top of our little refrigerator. Not an auspicious beginning, but I had not been told when they were to start.

When the Founder arrived, still in workout clothes, the consultants were all charmed with the Founder's tall tale that eight people jammed around a conference table was how Bill Gates got started. Project Mercury finally arrived and got credit for all the computer plugging in and networking that I had done. Then PTB arrived and gave them a yoga-Zen-love smile. I was exhausted and dirty, and it wasn't even lunch time.

As it turned out, the consulting software engineers were a great group of people. They were hard working, and I enjoyed them professionally as well as socially. Let's just say that the quality of my lunch hour really improved. The one problem appeared to be their Project Manager, a senior professional from the consulting firm we had hired. The Senior Engineer from the consulting company and one of the more junior programmers and I became good friends in the first couple of weeks they were in our office. At lunch, they both told me time and time again that their Project Manager was a joke and pulling the wool over the eyes of the Founder.

Their main argument seemed to be that there were roadblocks in the general design of the database that looked, to them, to be unsolvable. They were both concerned that the Founder's money and time were being greatly wasted, and they debated about what should be done. Should they inform the Project Manager who was their boss, or go around him and inform the Founder?

Finally, after much lunch time debate, the Senior Engineer decided to ask the Founder for a private meeting so he could explain the database problem. The Founder told the Senior Engineer, a technology professional with fourteen years of experience, that he, the Senior Engineer, was worried about nothing. Nothing? He just put his job and reputation on the line for nothing? It was unbelievable because the Founder was a remedial computer user at the time.

Little did the Senior Engineer know that the Founder was negotiating with this Project Manager to become our sixth employee. And within a few weeks, sure enough, we had one of our random staff meetings in which it was announced that the consulting company's Project Manager was now our Chief Technology Officer (CTO1) and was responsible for the architecture of the database they were building for us and the planning of the programming necessary to achieve the goals of the Company. My friends were horrified, and the Senior Engineer again put his job and reputation at risk by going back to his consulting company; there he spoke with his new supervisors about the database problem. He was told they would look into it, but that he likely had exaggerated. What a mess.

Six weeks passed, and the roadblocks that the Senior Engineer identified finally became apparent back at the consulting firm. There were angry meetings in which the Founder watched CTO1 defend himself and his database decisions to his colleagues at his old consulting company. In the face of clear evidence that there were problems with the database, the Founder stuck by CTO1, and refused to consider that much of anything could be wrong. Could it be that the Founder just couldn't see that CTO1 was a mistake, and was taking up our valuable resources including time, money and energy? Or maybe the Founder just couldn't admit to any hiring mistake?

In retrospect I can see the Founder's pattern here. Project Mercury and now CTO1 were both hiring errors. While Project Mercury was a relatively small drain on our resources and just an annoyance, hiring CTO1 was a critical financial and strategic mistake. This is what I learned from the early days:

- Everyone makes hiring mistakes so look clearly at your employees and assess if things are going the way you had planned when you hired them. Admitting mistakes early allows you to stop wasting money, Company resources, and enables you to get back on track.

- Good managers look at their employees objectively and assess performance accurately. Do not attribute the work of one individual to another. Everyone knows that this smoke screen is just the poor manager's way of covering up a staffing mistake and it fools no one.

- If people tell you that you have made a managerial mistake, consider seriously that they may be right. Sometimes people have your best interest at heart when they have the courage to disagree with you, let alone put their jobs and reputations on the line for your Company.

- Strong communication skills are critical to running a strong business.

- If you suspect an employee of substance abuse, confront the employee. Any kind of substance abuse hurts your other employees as well as the workplace itself.

Chapter 3: Entrepreneur Manure

Contributor: Vice President (VP) who was the Seventh Employee

---

Narrator: The Vice President (VP) had spent 30 years in the corporate world and was fascinated by the prospect of creating a new way of doing the core work of her industry. Here she describes the high energy and the brilliance of the vision of the Founder which lured the VP to the Company and the lessons that the VP learned about working with entrepreneurs.

Entrepreneur. What a great word. It feels good in the mouth, it rolls roundly off the tongue, and not just anyone can spell it. It is mysteriously part French and part Wall Street – not a common juxtaposition. The word *entrepreneur* had for me a wide range of associations. One image that topped my list was a visionary salesperson with high endless energy, and a laser focus on the finish line. But the dictionaries say that I am wrong because they, more or less collectively, define *entrepreneur* as one who "organizes and manages a business enterprise, assuming risk for profit." No mystery or romance there. But I had spent my career as an executive in corporations such as publicly traded retail chains, and as a teacher in colleges, and I had worked for a money management company that invested billions of dollars on behalf of pension funds. These are hardly hotbeds of entrepreneurship, by my definition anyway, so when the opportunity came to join a start-up company, I headed straight for the golden, entrepreneurial dream.

I became the Company's seventh employee when the group had been together for about six months. I was the Company's first Vice President (VP) and I was hired, to quote the Founder, "Because you know something about our primary industry, something about our secondary industry, and something about research." No one before, or after, has so succinctly summarized my 31-year career. But I was eager to witness and participate in entrepreneurship first hand, and I did not hesitate in the least to join the fledgling firm.

Let's return to my definition and compare it with my experience with the Founder and the Company. Was I right, or were the dictionaries?

Entrepreneur as Visionary: Nothing could be more true. The Founder had a vision for a new way of approaching the basic tasks of our industry and believed we could integrate a wide assortment of databases and automate what were currently very time consuming and boring tasks that were common but important and necessary in our industry. The goal was to replace intuition with science and improve the decision-making of our industry to avoid costly mistakes and optimize sales and profits   Our Founder was right about this initial vision.   These things were possible and the early adopters loved the fact that much of the risk in a serious and costly decision-making process was eliminated.   Our customers became dependent on our products to help them screen market opportunities.   Then we added an indexing system that enabled our customers to understand if their potential facilities were similar to their existing facilities. If they were similar, our customers then had an instant frame of reference, or metric, for assessing every new opportunity.

An industry that depended on "intuition" suddenly had an impartial metric that was so easy to use, we could, and did, train their inexperienced summer interns to use it.   And our customers loved us even more.   It was a heady and brilliant vision, indeed.

The Founder's vision extended to the delivery system for our products.   We embraced the Internet as our method to deliver products to our customers.   In our earliest days, the Internet was used for things such as obtaining news, processing business-to-consumer retail transactions, and stock trading.   There was very little business-to-business traffic when we started, although there were many positive media forecasts about the growth of our type of transaction.

This Internet component of the Founder's vision was also brilliant.   We developed our products as an ASP, or Application

Service Provider. This meant that the customer did not buy software in a shrink-wrapped box with tons of incorrect installation instructions and faulty data disks. They did not have to cajole their Information Technology (IT) department into installing it for them, nor did the IT department have to support it. Instead, we offered them stealth software. The software and data were housed on our servers, and the customer accessed them over the web using their password. For example, our customers would request data in the form of a report or map. That request would travel over the Internet to our computers where the data for that request would be assembled and sent back via the Internet to the customer, in one to four seconds. Multiple users could access the software from the field or from their hotel room, in fact anywhere that there was an Internet connection. In a sense, we became instant employees of our customers.

We supported the software ourselves, of course, but that also turned out to be brilliant, because we came to know the users of the products personally. Customer annual subscription renewals became almost automatic, because they knew us, trusted us, and had grown dependent on us as well as on our software. We knew what they loved about the products, and we could fix what they hated – quickly and without having to express mail another version of the software in a shrink-wrapped box. It was the most efficient way to use software that could be imagined at this time, and, for a while, it worked. So, yes, the Founder was a visionary.

Entrepreneur as Salesperson: Most definitely. There is almost something magical about the entrepreneur/salesperson who loves to work the sale. There can also be a negative side, however, in that all things are viewed as eternally negotiable, with the result that no good deal can ever be closed in a straightforward manner. Unfortunately, some of the sales pitches became intolerable, for example, if you sign a multi-year contract, (non-binding of course) we will give you a (binding) discount for the second year of the contract. Not interested in a multi-year contract? Well, then, how about giving us a testimonial and we will give you a 10% discount? You can't give us a testimonial because your in-house attorneys would have a fit? Well, then, how about letting us use your logo on the customer page of our web site? We will give you two months free access to our products in exchange. Sometimes the Founder negotiated brilliantly, but we wished it were for, rather than against our own Company. The Board, however, didn't see it this way and, with pride, called the Founder the "Rain Maker", "Deal Maker" or the "Closer".

Another attribute of the Founder as a true salesperson was that the adrenaline high of great drama was easily and constantly generated. I have seen the Founder simmer for forty-five minutes on the way to a venture capitalist's office, go into the rest room, come out composed, walk into the presentation with a million-dollar smile, get the venture capitalist's financial commitment, and then simmer all of the way back to the office because none of the employees could sell the way the Founder could. After several of these adventures, I came to suspect that for the Founder to function properly, life on the edge was a requirement. Simmering on the way down to a meeting was to be the precursor to the tragedy that they might say "no" and the repercussions of rejection would be overwhelming. Simmering on the way back was from relief that they said "yes". Often, we barely escaped complete and total disaster through the unimaginable, heroic, adrenaline-fed negotiations of the Founder.

The Founder also shared another attribute of the true salesperson which is the inability to hear "no." The Founder could say "no" but could not hear "no." The Founder would circle around and approach the prospective client from a different angle, again and again and again, as long as the prospect would allow it. And sometimes the prospect would allow it for months (you prospects know who you are, so get some backbone). In many ways, the Founder redefined persistence, which of course was fine if you were watching, but horrifying if you were the potential customer. But the Founder's prospect-to-customer conversion rate was excellent in the early days. We often got tired, hungry, and battered customers, many of whom were yearning to be free even as they signed a (non-binding) multi-year contract. Our job was to love the customer who had just been wrestled to the ground and get them to love us back. Our great products helped us do just that.

Entrepreneur = High Endless Energy: No question. The energy flowed twenty-four hours a day, seven days a week before 24/7 was invented. It was wonderful when it manifested itself in the relentless pursuit of investors. In the beginning the Founder's high energy was good for office morale and productivity. An enthusiastic laugh from the Founder coming up the stairs was the starting point of our day.

But high energy, we came to understand, also meant that the Founder would leave us voice and e-mail messages at 12:30am, 3:00am and 6:30am, on the same day. It also meant that two people would be asked to do the same task, because a back-up employee might understand better than the original employee how critically important the task was and might finish it faster. But most important, high energy meant the Founder perceived multi-tasking as a personal talent. For example, the Founder would give a sales pitch on the phone while tracking the stock market or reading e-mail. The Founder felt writing (not reading) another new business plan for the Company while on the Stairmaster was productive and became annoyed when the executive-assistant-du-jour could not decipher the scribbled notes. The Founder and I had two, entire restaurant dinners during which we did not exchange a single word because the Founder was on the cell phone to the Chairman and taking notes on a laptop computer. The Founder was a new definition of high energy for me.

<u>Entrepreneur with Laser Focus:</u>   This laser focus was strangely missing and there are books that can guide and instruct entrepreneurs on this very topic. Moore's *Crossing the Chasm* addresses the intense market-focus a company such as ours needed. How easy it must have been for the Founder to believe that failure

was impossible for a high-energy person with a brilliant idea for which the Founder successfully raised money against all odds because our industry was in a tough investment climate. To laser focus on your Company, your product, your competitors, and your industry, and to make very hard strategic decisions in the relative dark because you are, after all, doing something no one has done before must be terrifying. And then the Founder had to live with those decisions.

In retrospect, after two years or so it became easier for the Founder to embrace the Chairman's philosophy which was to "throw everything against the wall and see what sticks" rather than to chart a clear course and be held responsible for the results. The theory was that one could not be held responsible for unforeseen perils. But this sort of "wall-sticking" behavior, according to collective dictionaries, is not entrepreneurial. Our Board of Directors should have known this and corrected it but did not.

So rather than quibble with the collective dictionaries or discard my wonderful and utopian original definition of *entrepreneur,* I have evolved it to my current definition of the term *successful entrepreneur.* The entrepreneur is a great gift to the business world, but that person may also be the most serious challenge to your company. Entrepreneurs are giant contributors with fantastic personalities and incredibly upbeat outlooks. But in order to keep them productive and positively involved they must be kept focused. This is what I learned about working with an entrepreneur:

- An entrepreneur usually starts with a great vision, a wonderful idea. But it may take more than one incredible idea for the Company to ultimately succeed, so the successful entrepreneur must keep thinking and must keep creating. The entrepreneur must also learn to listen to and allow employees and customers to have their own incredible ideas because the Company will need those ideas to be successful.

- An entrepreneur who is a good salesperson is the dream of most small companies; even better is a salesperson focused on obtaining key customers who generate industry chatter about your new company and its amazing products. Better still are the salespeople who listen to the customers and feed all of their customers good ideas back into the Company and its products. Best, is the salesperson who builds relationships with customers, so that they want and need the Company to succeed and are personally bound to the Company.

- The endless energy of the Founder/entrepreneur is essential to the start-up business because the work is long and hard. The trick is to focus the Founder's energy on the mission of the Company and to not let them expend it in any other way. Do not let them chase every opportunity, every strategic alliance, or partnership, and do not enable them to explore every avenue they think of at 2:00am because it will take too long to identify which ones are losers. And if you, as a Founder, hear not one but a chorus of Twilight Zone theme songs from your employees when you mention your newest opportunity, strategic alliance, or partnership, listen to them. They may be doing you a gigantic favor.

- There may be no more important message to the future successful entrepreneur than to develop a laser focus on your employees, your competition, your customers, your products, and your business environment. Can the entrepreneur really focus on all the things that need intense concentration? Probably not, but employees were created for this reason. Find the best employees you can and tell them what to focus on so that everyone spends time rowing, rather than bailing out the Company canoe.

Maybe the best advice I can give the entrepreneur is to quote Harvey Penick, the great golf teacher and coach, who insisted, "Take dead aim."

Chapter 4: How I Spent My High School Internship

Contributor: High School Intern

> **Narrator:** *The high school Intern was a bright, self-deprecating and wise-beyond-her-years sixteen-year-old. She came on board with great enthusiasm for the work of the Company and quickly became familiar with our challenging software that enabled her to be an excellent contributor. With no business experience she quickly figured out the very important basics of successfully running a start-up business. Her final internship presentation was bold and crammed full of essentials for business success.*

On my way to work that first morning, my knuckles were white and my palms sweaty as my hands gripped the steering wheel. My car sped down the highway as dark clouds hung heavily in the sky. Rain poured down in sheets. The wind, rushing down the hillsides, forced the rain to beat incessantly against the car. The windshield blurred. Ahead the highway became an urgent river. The sweeping image of our local mountain, which usually appeared above the tidal flats, was hidden from my view in a swirling gray envelope of rain and wind. It was a dark and stormy morning.

Having received my driver's license a few weeks earlier and not having any experience driving on the freeway in such formidable weather, I was, to say the least, terrified. And if my fear of hydroplaning, spinning out of control, and driving off the edge of the freeway overpass into the murky salt marshes were not enough, today was my first day of work at the Company. I was doubly terrified but excited. I knew that the door of opportunity was opening wide for me because the prospect of an internship at a software development dot.com was rare for high school students. Especially in my hometown which was the opposite of Silicon Valley. The idea of working at a dot.com, which was at the time the most innovative and prominent type of company, was also intimidating. I knew the Company employed some of the most intelligent and well-known business professionals on the West Coast, and I, a lowly sixteen-year-old, would be working for them.

I took a deep breath as I pulled my beat-up gray minivan into the Company parking lot. The lot was filled with new cars: BMWs, several Mercedes and sporty little Volkswagens. I decided to park my hand-me-down Plymouth Voyager family van in the least conspicuous spot possible. Before heading into the office, my mind wandered back to my first introduction to the Company.

As a high school junior, I had enrolled in a program offered by my school called Academy X. The Academy functioned as a school within the larger high school. With a group of fifty other students, I took courses in English, History, and Workplace Learning, all of which were integrated. Holistically, the classes focused on community involvement and professional development. We learned about interpersonal communication and public speaking, presentation strategies and professionalism. The central aspect of the academy was our four-month internship. Tuesdays and Thursdays were devoted entirely to our internship. It was a pretty good deal. What high school student wouldn't want to escape the monotony of classes and the social pettiness of high school corridors?

I was interested in business, especially in data research, and wanted an internship in that field. I was also interested in learning how a small business operates. My dad, an architect, heard about an up-and-coming data research firm and knew their Executive Vice President of Sales and Marketing, the EVP. My dad spoke with the EVP who advised that I contact the Founder directly. It took me a couple of days to get up my courage because I was only 16. When I finally phoned the Founder, I was hastily directed to the Vice President (VP). Finally, I was talking to the right person! And I could not believe that my very first try at "networking" worked!

The VP spoke quickly and succinctly. No chit chat. This caught me off guard and, although it was surprising, it was understandable. I wasn't accustomed to the speed of business, especially business based on the Internet. The line I remember hearing most around that time was: the Internet is increasing the speed of business. I knew that advances in communication technologies and computer products had created an influx of venture capitalists looking to invest in all of these businesses. The business community was in a frenzy to catch the investment wave. My initial contact with the Company and my interview with the VP confirmed what I had heard about the Internet start-up company culture. Fast-paced and exciting, it doesn't stop for anyone. My interview was set up after I faxed in my resume and cover letter.

On my way into the unimpressive building that housed my future workplace, I checked my reflection in the glass doors; the Company logo obstructed my reflection a bit. Wearing my black cargo skirt and jean jacket, I wasn't exactly the image of corporate chic, but this wasn't exactly your standard corporate firm. All dot-comers wear Levis or khakis, or so I hoped. Although it is now almost four years since that interview, everyone tells me my appearance hasn't changed much. That is hardly the case. I remember myself as an acne-ridden teen with scraggly blonde hair that *never* did what I wanted it to do (no matter how much I tried). I was a dork, I knew it, but I was now a dork who was going after an internship! I was a dot.com dork embarking on what I thought might be a career path – and that made me feel just slightly cooler.

At the top of the stairs the second-floor office spread out spaciously before me. Directly in front was the receptionist's desk, to the right large cubicles in an L-shape, to the left a large conference table, beyond that, two or three big desks. The office seemed surprisingly empty. The only person in sight was the receptionist who sat quietly at her computer. The large desks were not cluttered with papers, folders or anything like that. One desk held an unplugged meditation fountain. I introduced myself, and the receptionist directed me toward the conference table. As I made my way over, I saw that there actually *were* people in the office, all tucked away neatly in their cubby hole desks. Almost immediately the VP emerged from the row of large cubicles – a Diet Coke, complete with straw, in hand. The VP smiled when she saw me staring at the Diet Coke (it was only 8:30am!!) and she explained that it was the real breakfast of champions. Whatever!

Unlike her haste on the phone, the VP seemed calm today. It must be a slow day at the office, or at least I hoped so. My interview consisted mainly of the VP explaining what the Company was about, its history, vision, and office culture. It sounded like she was selling the business to me, as if I was an investor or client. Maybe the VP was just practicing her sales pitch, or maybe she was still trying to sell the Company to herself. Either way, all I knew was she didn't need to sell me anything. This was the coolest, well actually the *only*, job interview I had ever had. As long as they wanted me, I was going to take the internship. The VP explained that I would have to be flexible – you never knew what task might come up. I put in that that was just fine, Academy X requires us to be flexible, too.

I was surprised when at the end of our meeting the VP, without hesitation, told me that they would love to have me as an intern. Was I that impressive? Couldn't be. But what start-up business, over loaded with work and deadlines, could say no to free labor? I was happy to oblige.

During the first four months of the internship phase, I settled quickly into the routine of office work. I worked on address data collection for our proprietary database making sure the address latitude and longitude coordinates were in an accurate and readable format. I swapped data files with the Director of Data, with whom the VP also worked closely, and then formatted and input the data into a database.

And, I was also in charge of maintaining a database that tracked the Company's competing firms. I spent a lot of my time in this task searching the web, looking for information on other Internet-based firms in the data research industry. Early on, it became clear to me that no other company was providing the service we were developing. This realization - that we were going it alone and blazing a new trail - made me both excited and nervous.

Would the Company succeed? Was there really a demand for our products? If there was demand, will we start a new trend in organizing and accessing data? The Company certainly had a unique product, but the product development team, of which I was a part, was walking blindly. I cannot repeat enough times just how intelligent all the employees were. But intelligence isn't everything. We were taking a big risk, and it seemed that everyone understood it. The possibility of success infused the firm with excitement, yet the possibility of failure always lurked not far behind. During my time at the Company, questions of the Company's future were always in the back of my mind. Suddenly I was interested in more than just the dynamics of a small business operation; I wanted to see how the Company's future unfolded.

Not only was my competition spreadsheet used for internal purposes, as I thought it would be, but it also ended up being shown to potential investors as part of the Company's business presentation. When the VP told me this news I was very happy – *my* work could possibly contribute to successful fund raising for the Company. On one occasion, the Founder hosted an open house for a number of wealthy individuals known as angel investors. When one of them asked if the Company had done any research on their competition and if the Company knew the market they were entering, the Founder was able to pull out my file. The investors were impressed that the Company had taken time to understand the industry, and they used my information to judge whether the Company would be successful or not!

This mini-story taught me a few things about the basics of starting a business. First, I realized that one of the most crucial factors in starting a company is getting investors. A software company needs capital for start-up operations such as product development, marketing, and all other costs incurred in business.

Second, I learned that in order to obtain investments a company needs to meet certain criteria set by its investors. The Company needed to have a strong product, a strong team and "proof" of future profitability. My competition spreadsheet was one piece of that proof.

A third lesson I learned is that the search for financing goes on *before* the product is even complete. Going into my internship, I had expected that the Company would have already created the software they were selling. The Founder, however, was promoting a product that was not even complete. In fact, sometimes I wondered if it was even possible to create the flawless software application the Founder led the investors to expect. For example, while working on the product development side of the business, I was surprised that the pre-existing data sources we were using in the databases were flawed. Getting addresses to map accurately was quite an undertaking. The sheer number of addresses, hundreds of thousands, made it a never-ending project.

In my naiveté, I had assumed that the world outside of school, *especially* the business world, would run efficiently, and that this type of information would be easily accessible and always accurate. I couldn't have been more wrong. The Company's product development phase required an enormous amount of critical thinking and problem solving, which I have come to understand is a substantial part of doing business in general. This distinguishes one firm from another: the firm's ability to deal with dilemmas in a timely and effective manner. Whenever I came across a problem that seemed unfixable with the database, the VP had a solution or would develop a new strategy to solve the problem. Investment is a crucial factor of business success, but so is product development led by a team of dedicated and passionate employees.

Besides the hard work, there was some fun, too. One of my favorite and most vivid memories of the Company was our trip to the industry's convention. This convention, a huge, four-day long exhibition, involved everyone in our industry. It was decided that this convention would be the stage for the Company's big product launch. The whole Company was buzzing with plans for our introduction to the larger world.

I remember that during the months leading up to the convention our Marketing Maven was crazed with marketing projects. She was creating postcards for mass mailings, mini-discs that were both business cards and a multimedia introduction to the Company, ads for industry magazines and plans for marketing at the convention itself. She set up meeting and dinner appointments where the sales people could sell our products, just as the Founder had done with angel investors. A big party was planned for the first night of the convention. The Company would provide a good time for all along with an excellent chance to network. The Founder was constantly doing media interviews, and the Company was written up in a number of different publications – all in an effort to increase Company visibility. The Company seemed to be, or at least it was marketed as, one of the most exciting and innovative new companies in our industry.

On the other side of the office, the VP and her team, myself included, continued to work on the databases and product layouts to make sure they were ready for the convention. We were under a giant deadline to get the website and products up and running. Investors, apparently, did not need to see a finished product, but customers did. To make sure that our products were as attractive and clear as possible, I set up a bulletin board covered with competitor products that I had found on different websites with categories such as "Products We Like," "OK Products," and "Products We Hate." We incorporated and improved on aspects of the "Products We Like" and made sure not to make the mistakes of the hated products – like maps that used mud brown, slimy yellow and small print.

Thanks to all the preparation, the convention went off without a hitch. I arrived the second day of the convention and was greeted with stories of the riotous party the night before when, unfortunately, the Founder had fallen and broken a foot. Well, OK, there was that one hitch. Most of my time at the convention was spent walking around the exhibition halls, enjoying the free Starbucks beverages and checking out the competition in person rather than on the web. Even wearing my crisp white shirt, with Company logo in the right corner, I felt underdressed. I was swimming in a sea of suits. Businessmen, and I do mean business*men,* the business*women* were few and far between, had come from all over the country to wheel and deal. And I thought times had changed. Whatever. Our convention was clearly dominated by good-ole-boy vibes. Our Company, a small Internet start-up staffed 50% by smart women, was clearly not the status quo, and it may even have been the only tech-company in attendance.

At the end of my internship I had to give a Power Point presentation in front of the whole Company plus my internship teacher from my school. This presentation had to state what my teacher called the Focus Question and had to summarize my responsibilities during the internship and the key lessons that I learned. The VP was not allowed to help me – this was my project the whole way.

Here is my Focus Question, how I answered it and what I learned on my Internship.

Focus Question: **What does it take to successfully launch a start-up company?**

My Internship Discoveries:

1. Problem solving is an incredibly important skill.

2. Business itself is a web – every person in the Company relies on one another.

What It Takes for a Company to Succeed:

1. Money

2. Successful product development

3. Strong technology

4. Targeted marketing

5. Dedication and passion

6. A strong team

Do you have what it takes?

1. Yes, skills and knowledge

2. Dedication (yes, I listed this twice because I had not anticipated how much dedication is   necessary for a company to be successful)

3. Problem solving skills (yes, twice!)

4. Flexibility – yes on this.

These are the lessons I learned during my high school internship with the Company. And, very cool, I got an A!!

Chapter 5: Lights, Camera, Friction

Contributor: The Second Receptionist

Narrator: *The Second Receptionist (of six receptionists in four years) was a hard-working, humorous, flexible person who could multi-task with the best of them. She worked with the Founder's executive assistants (there were five in four years) to coordinate Board packages and meetings, plan external sales pitches and marketing materials, make daily revisions to the business plan and schedule potential investor meetings, in addition to working on special projects and, yes, being the Company receptionist. Her interaction with the Founder was intense. Our receptionist typically started the day cheerfully, was bemused by noon, irritated by 2:30pm and homicidal by 6:00pm. When she left the Company, we lost a solid rock and the Founder's chaos caught an updraft.*

I love the theater and, I am a bit embarrassed to admit, I am very comfortable with theatrics. I was in my first play when I was fourteen. The play was *Sweeny Todd: The Demon Barber of Fleet Street*, but without singing to ensure that we would have an audience. I played one of Sweeny's victims, but who didn't? Sweeny routinely slit my throat about half way through the play each night. I had such a crush on Sweeny! He was so good looking that any girl who was even close to room temperature had a crush on him. But I ramble. I have had a long association with the theater as my avocation and, you could argue, it should have prepared me for the drama of the Founder.

It took me a while to put my finger on the correct theater analogy to describe my working relationship with the Founder. To say it was like a play, demeans the art. To say it was like the circus, denigrates the trained and disciplined animals. It was too unreal to be a reality show. To suggest it was like a sitcom, is close but still a bit off. Finally, I realized what it was; I was the supporting actress in the Founder's show. Yes, that captures it exactly.

The spot lights, flood lights, orchestra lights, house lights, marquee lights, all lights were on the Founder. We were not just employees; we were the Founder's tools/servants/props/scenery and audience. Much of this behavior can be credited to the fact that the Founder was, indeed, the Founder and felt entitled to the scenery and audience. In most businesses that would not be an issue because there would be a professional manager who would direct the work of the company and dilute the effect of a one-person show. After raising the necessary funds, shouldn't the role of the Founder be to appear at monthly staff lunches, heartily thank the little people for fulfilling the business dream, and then exit stage right to great applause?

When I joined the Company it was small, just fourteen employees, and the Founder was not to be up-staged. Now, let me give you a few examples so that you will not accuse me of being too theatrical.

We had an open office. It was the full floor, 1,500 square feet, of an industrial building and there were no walls. Everyone could hear just about everything. The Founder liked to go for a morning run or have an early workout and then arrive at the office about 9:30am in exercise shorts and damp t-shirt to use the shower in the bathroom at the back of our floor. The minute the Founder would enter the shower/bathroom, I would hold my breath because the material generated from that room was priceless. For example, there was the morning that the Founder was running late for a meeting at our office. The gentleman the Founder was to meet was already seated opposite me in the reception area and I had given him a cup of black, hot coffee, when the phone rang. I answered with the Company name, as you would expect. From the shower the Founder was calling me on the cell phone to tell me that the gentleman sitting across from me was going to arrive at any moment and would I please entertain him. He could hear the Founder's booming voice both from the shower and through my headset while I tried to look invisible.

On another morning, after another shower, the Founder was running late for yet another meeting in our office and left the shower in a hurry. I got a call on the cell phone from our conference room table, which was only twenty feet away, in the middle of that meeting telling me that the Founder's sweaty shorts and a sweaty t-shirt had inadvertently been left over the top of the shower door. I was told to retrieve them and to take them down to the trunk of the Founder's car. This type of personal, boundaryless behavior happened with some regularity.

The shower was also perceived as the Founder's office space. One afternoon I seriously needed to use the rest room, if you know what I mean. Not thinking ahead, I walked in and locked the door. Several minutes later the Founder came looking for me – yes, I was in the rest room. My stall door was still closed, as were my eyes, and the Founder stood outside the restroom and told me the next three things I needed to do, one of which was get the Founder's car washed, when I was "done." Obviously, I had nothing to take notes on, but my training as an actress had given me a good memory.

But there was much more than just bathroom humor working for the Founder. Often there were meetings outside the office to which the Founder typically ran late. Well, running late was standard operating procedure because the Founder was stretched thin and extremely busy and wanted you to know it. When the Founder would get into the car, I would hold my breath. The phone would ring usually before the parking lot had been exited. What was the street address of the company where the meeting was being held? Thanks, click. The phone would ring again. Go on-line to Map Quest and read the driving instructions to the company where the meeting was being held. Thanks, click. The phone would ring. Was that a right or left on Main Street? OK, click. Did I know if there was a parking lot? OK, click. Could I call them and tell them there was an accident on the highway and that the Founder was going to be fifteen minutes late? Click.

This was the Founder's standard going-to-my-meeting behavior. You may be wondering if anyone else ever attended those meetings with the Founder. Anyone that was also to join the meeting from our office would typically take all the meeting materials and leave twenty minutes before the Founder. Somehow when the other employees left the parking lot I never had the same sense of anticipation that I did with the Founder. Of course, there was the day when on the third or fourth phone call I could hear boisterous expletives as the Founder rear-ended someone. That was the last call that day, and, funny, the accident was never mentioned to me after that.

This behavior, while great material for a book or sitcom, had the predictable negative effect over the long term of eroding morale at all levels in the Company. Oddly, or so I thought initially, it also had the effect of throwing our seasoned, experienced professionals a bit off center. I overheard them wondering, "When do you think the Founder will get to the meeting? Should we start without the Founder? Should we begin by introducing the Company and our credentials and maybe by then the Founder will have arrived? How road-raged, pre-occupied, watch-watching will the Founder be during the meeting?" Over time, I noticed that these other senior people routinely made "Plan B" for any presentation, sales pitch or investor presentation. Now it seems to me, if I were on-stage and did not know if the star was going to get to the theater before the second act, that would negatively shade my performance. But these people were professionals and they dealt with this uncertainty fairly well, though constantly looking over their shoulders to gauge where and how the Founder was must have been difficult. And then there were the Founder's personal chores as I:

- Dropped off and picked up the Founder's visiting aged mother at the hairdresser,

- Chose and picked up hors d'oeuvres for a personal party the Founder gave at home,

- Called the exterminator numerous times so they would place extra poison in the Founder's office area when we had a family of rats in the rafters.

Please keep in mind that the Founder had an Executive Assistant, or fixer/handler as we used to say, and every time I left my desk to do things for the Founder someone else with a higher salary had to do my nominal job. Certainly, if you are the founder, president, or CEO you can send anyone in the company to do errands for you – you are the boss. But here is the message that you convey to the rest of the company when you do this:

- Part of this company exists for my personal convenience; therefore, the company's mission statement should include making me happy,

- Since some employees are here for my happiness, the rest of you will just have to pick up the slack when that employee is off doing her real job of making me happy.

This results in the corporate phone being answered by the Part-Time Bookkeeper, or by whoever else is around. It also means that the Vice President of Sales will probably have to do more copying and collating than he ever dreamed of and this will not make him productive or happy. It means that an intense product development meeting will be interrupted when the VP has to sign for a Fed Ex package. Are these big deals? No, but over time the constant interruptions wear people down and erode morale. It is your prerogative – if you are the boss – but am I doing my job and contributing to the workflow of your business, or am I getting your car washed? Really, it's your call. So here is what I learned working for the Founder:

- If time management is a problem at the top levels, then, please, consider getting some training for those executives, regardless of their titles. Lack of good time management does not affect just these executives. It negatively affects the other people with whom they work.

- Find another way of generating adrenaline, if it takes adrenaline to get you moving, instead of running late for every meeting. Running late does not imply that you are a very busy person. It is my observation that truly busy, effective people respect time, both yours and theirs.

- My six-year-old niece can use GPS and the Founder who started a tech company can't? Really?

- If you are the boss, let your employees do their jobs and get someone else to help you with your personal errands. Doing this shows respect for your Company and your employees and indicates that you understand priorities.

Chapter 6: The Heartbreaking Tale of Successfully Developing Our Web Products

Contributor: Vice President (VP)

Narrator: *The VP was a seasoned professional who joined the Company with great enthusiasm and energy because she deeply believed in the products the Founder wanted to develop for their industry. The VP was a logical, common sense, team player. She was a good person to have around if you were attempting something for the first time because she was a strong problem solver. She should have been a highly valued employee based on her contributions to the development of the web products, yet the Founder and the Chairman preferred the counsel of employees who had little or no industry experience.*

I love a good challenge and something that has never been done before, with an impossible deadline, with people who have never worked together and who have wildly different backgrounds is my definition of a good challenge. And so, when the Founder described just this type of job to me it was inevitable that I would say yes.

My first role in the Company as the Vice President (VP) was to take the Founder's initial idea and expand it into a suite of products that our future customers would access over the Internet. I was to work with the consulting software engineers and bring the first set of products to fruition in eleven months for launch at our biggest industry annual convention. No one had products like the ones we were going to build – we were going to be the first in our industry and we had forty-seven weeks to do it. I loved the challenge.

My first week with the Company was a bit weird. First, I learned that the Founder had a rocky professional relationship and a vague scope of work with the outside consulting company whose software engineers were working with us to build the first suite of products.

Second, there was a giant white board in CTO1's office with the flow chart of the architecture of the software that we were to develop drawn in various colored markers. This flow chart was the centerpiece and focus of the weekly product development meetings. On this schema there were drawn, in among the other things, five red circles with the letters AMOH inside each circle. Since my work for the Company was a new application of my professional experience, I did not hesitate to ask questions when I ran into something that stumped me as this did. AMOH stands for, it was explained to me, A Miracle Occurs Here. Translated this means that CTO1 had no idea how to resolve these key roadblocks but hoped the solutions would appear when needed. These troublesome issues aside, however, we had deadlines to meet so the consulting software engineers and I got down to work.

CTO1 had perfectly groomed, gleaming white hair and a Buddha smile. He came to work around 9:30am and left at 4:30pm due to his long commute. He also worked from home on Friday as an additional accommodation for the long commute. CTO1 had previously led and managed software development teams of up to 150 people for the US military. The consulting software engineers the Company had contracted with included one Egyptian, two Pakistanis, a couple of Americans, and one Australian. We were the entire software development team. This was only the second time I had worked professionally with software engineers and I found them smart, hardworking, and very serious. I had been hired to provide the team with the industry knowledge, or "domain expertise," and I answered all of their business-related questions for the future products.

Our team had an unusual combination of skills and backgrounds, but we were united in our desire to do this thing that no one had done before. We started work at about 7:00am each day, spent the first thirty minutes discussing problems, did heads down work until a twenty-minute lunch and then did heads down work until 7:00pm, Monday through Saturday. It was a very focused work environment and resulted in intense work relationships and odd experiences. For example, the Senior Engineer was a young man born in Egypt and educated in Great Britain. He and I had roughly the same sense of humor and we got along well. We had been working very hard to get the data for the first product correct for about three weeks and one afternoon he called me to the printer when he thought that we finally had it right. As the first report rolled successfully off the printer we both had tears in our eyes and the rest of the team made us take a victory lap. This first report looked nothing like the ultimate finished product but it was, in many ways, proof-of-concept, and we were ecstatic.

Approximately five weeks later it became painfully clear that arrows and mathematical formulas indicating resolutions were not replacing the red AMOHs on the flow chart. The Founder had repeatedly assured our Board of Directors that product development was on schedule but now it was apparent even to the Board that something was wrong. At an emergency Board meeting CTO1 was removed when he could no longer explain the slipping deadlines and the consulting engineers were dismissed. This left us with a constructed database but no way for it to be used because the consultants did not have the development of the user interface in the contract the Founder had negotiated.

By now the relationship between the Founder and the outside consultants had deteriorated so dramatically that the consultants had no intention of bidding on and building this, shall we say, essential user interface. So, the database was like a roast turkey in an oven that has no handle on the door. You could see the turkey, you could smell the turkey, and you knew the turkey had the potential to taste good, but you could not slice and eat the turkey as there was no way to open the oven and get to the turkey. We now had twenty-eight weeks until our convention.

CTO1 was replaced by CTO2, who was an acquaintance of the Founder. CTO2 was extremely bright, had a quick laugh and a free spirit. When he came on board the two of us worked hard and fast going over the product specifications and prototypes in preparation for the next development team. We worked on terminology and relationships between the pieces of our complex assignment. We expanded our data sets and refined our proprietary algorithms.

CTO2 and the new Chief Engineer quickly assembled the second development team. It consisted of the Chief Engineer, who had worked with CTO2 in the past on consulting projects, five software engineers whom the Chief Engineer had hired, and me. CTO2 and I were based in the West Coast office but the rest of the team was based in Utah, and it was patiently explained to me that this would be more efficient as the engineers would not have to put up with the Founder's amazing ability to generate chaos. We began anew; there were now twenty-four weeks before our convention.

The Chief Engineer was tall, slim and from an eastern European country. He shaved his head and smiled like Jack Nicholson, when he smiled at all. He prided himself on being smarter than everyone and to give him credit, between him and CTO2, there were no AMOHs on their flow chart.

The second team of software engineers was composed of an interesting collection of hard working, smart young men. The whole team focused on performance, which meant how quickly could the computers return the answer to the customer's query for data. The products became very fast and very impressive. Again, we worked twelve-hour days and six days a week.

The intense relationship I had with the original group of consulting engineers did not form between me and the Utah engineers because of the physical distance between us; there were no tearful scenes by the printer. There was, however, a real sense of excitement for all of us in breaking new ground and it bound us loosely together. The engineers built products to our business specifications and created a user interface so we could finally feast on that turkey. We tested the user interface, tested the products, and de-bugged our system. Five days before our convention deadline the first products were demonstrated to the whole company and we were given a standing ovation. We were ready, with just days to spare, to stun our industry at the convention.

We gave 302 product demonstrations on the convention trade show floor! We were hoarse, exhilarated, proud, and running on 100% adrenaline. The products were generating tremendous interest and excitement. People often stood three and four deep around our booth to watch a demonstration. It was incredibly satisfying, both professionally and personally. We could see, in the not too distant future, Success.

After the convention we had filled a three-ring binder with business cards from potential customers. The plan was to refine and continue to de-bug the products (in three intense weeks) and then set up and give product demonstrations to the most likely and most desirable potential clients. These we defined as leading edge companies that would generate positive word-of-mouth advertising for us. The goal was to get these targeted customers to agree to beta test the products for us. Beta testing allows the customer a sneak preview of an unreleased product and would, we hoped, get some of these targets hooked.

It worked. We converted half of our product demonstrations into beta testers and half of our beta testers into paying subscribers. We were told by our Chairman, who was also an investor in our Company, that our beta period was "flawless" and that our beta-test-to-customer conversion ratio was phenomenal. We gladly believed him.

Fifteen months had now elapsed since my first week. The work, the people and the pace were all more challenging than I had originally anticipated, but we had a solid start on the first suite of products and we had great customers who were eager for the second product suite. We began the push to the next launch of complementary products. The twelve-hour work days resumed.

My small team had been working on the prototypes for the second suite of products for about four months. We quickly finished them and handed them off to CTO2, the Chief Engineer and our software developers in Utah. Simultaneous with this product prototype transfer to the engineers there was a company cash crisis. With all of the product pressure and the financial problems in the West Coast office no one noticed the silence from Utah.

In late December, we got a first look at the second suite of products – those that we now had three weeks to de-bug before beta testing with our now enthusiastic customers. The whole development team, with the Founder and the Chairman, had made the decision months earlier to develop this second suite of products on industry-standard software. At the command of the Chief Engineer, however, the Utah software engineers ignored this decision and built the products using open source code.

Open source was a hip, underground-ish software code obtainable for "free" on the Internet. It was created and maintained by a community of programmers who disliked the tyranny and the sameness of large software companies. This body of programmers believed software should be universally available and accessible to all who need it, much like clean air.

The rationale used for Utah's decision to abandon the industry standard software as the basis for this next set of products was, I am sure you guessed, that open source code is "free." The Utah team obsequiously referenced the recent Company cash crisis and noted that they had saved the Company money because they had used open source code, which has no annoying licensing fee.

The Utah team, they hinted, was composed of Company heroes for their courageous programming effort.

Unfortunately, this second suite of products was far more complex than the first and required expertise that was built into the industry standard software but not into open source code. By using open source code, the Utah team had had to dumb down the product features because the engineers themselves did not have the necessary knowledge or time to develop products that could directly compete with those built with the standard, licensed software. These open source products did not look like the prototypes we had given the Utah office nor did they behave like them, and the user interface had to be entirely re-created. Additionally, several important products had not been developed because the Chief Engineer did not personally see the need for them.

Well, many say that the best things in life are "free." Perhaps. But in this situation what was saved in licensing fees was spent three times over in redesign and de-bugging time, loss of trust between the West Coast and Utah offices, and immeasurable stress in the West Coast office. The Chief Engineer had, in essence, scrapped all of the work we, the business side of the development team, had handed them. But knowing that time is money and that money often meant paychecks, we swallowed most of our anger and de-bugged this second product suite while the Utah office grudgingly added the missing products. It was teamwork under the worst conditions.

Oddly, I kept waiting for the moment when the Founder, the Chairman, CTO2, the Chief Engineer and I would gather around the speakerphone and discuss the problems that arise when the technology people make business decisions. I thought this conversation might also include a general discussion of the Company hierarchy because, as it appeared to me, the Chief Engineer had gone off in the direction of open source code without telling his boss, CTO2. I further conjectured the Chairman might mention during this phone call that the second suite of products was not competitive with many of the other products built on standard software because it did not include all of the capabilities our end users would require. On this phone call, I also envisioned that the Chairman, who told us he had thirty years of experience in the software development business, might express his disappointment in the decisions and actions of the Chief Engineer.

Needless to say, this fantasy phone call did not take place. Why? The Founder and the Chairman knew so little about this second, complex set of products that they never understood that by switching to open source code, the Chief Engineer, who told them that this was a necessary technology decision, was in effect making a business decision that disadvantaged our product's capabilities. The Founder and the Chairman bought into the brilliance of the Chief Engineer's technology decision without understanding that he had developed products that did not have the basic functionality our industry would expect. For whatever reason, they had to believe that the Chief Engineer was a genius and they refused to see that, genius notwithstanding, he just might be a hiring mistake.

In this grueling, professional environment we were still able to convert 28% of our second, larger group of beta testers to paid subscribers by promising short-term product "enhancements" to the second suite of products, accompanied by price reductions for the customers. A veneer of Company calm existed briefly.

Then, several days after the final beta tester had been converted to a paying customer there was an impromptu conference call in the Founder's office. Maybe this was the conference call I irrationally still expected?

The Chairman ran the multi-office call and started it by reiterating that in his thirty years in the software business he had never seen two flawless, back-to-back, beta test periods like ours (we glowed). He continued that he had never seen tester-to-customer conversion rates as high as ours (we GLOWED). He acknowledged that, although we had had our differences, we worked around them and then he praised the Utah office. The Chairman said they were the best software developers he had ever worked with and that the Chief Engineer was a star (glow fades). Then he thanked the Utah office and hung up.

The Chairman then turned to the rest of us and stated that we (a new company with great clients, growing revenue and an incomplete product offering) were not going to do any more software development. We were to halt the product development schedule in mid-stream.

CTO2 and I exchanged bewildered looks. This was an astonishing conclusion for the Chairman to reach. Against all odds, and under the most bizarre company structure, we had put most of our emotions aside and had worked as a team. We, and our customers, needed the immediate, promised, product enhancements, then we needed to push to the third suite of products to remain as far out in front of our competitors as possible. CTO2 and I were allowed no input into this fundamentally wrong business decision.

CTO2 resigned two weeks later. The Chief Engineer became CTO3 and the rest of the development team, including me, remained intact and employed. There was no more product development but there were no layoffs and no cost savings. What was the point of this decision? Were the Founder and the Chairman afraid of success? Why halt product development yet realize no cost savings by not laying off the team? What in the world was the Chairman thinking, and why did the Founder agree with him? We never learned the basis for the Chairman's wild decision but it held for eighteen months.

And then, our competitors began to develop their own web-based products.

Where to start with the lessons? This experience was good and not good but let me try to distill the more important lessons:

- Many companies have an organizational chart for a reason. Individuals who do not appear to understand the company structure and hierarchy should be softly spoken to, nonstop, until they get it. No senior executive should let anyone get away with the ridiculous behavior of our Chief Engineer.

- Senior executives need to pay more attention to what is really going on in their company. Calling a business decision a technology decision, and then allowing the tech people to get away with it, only demonstrates that senior management has but a patina of industry knowledge.

- Senior managers can and will make bad business decisions based on apparently irrational emotions. As an employee, do not waste your time trying to understand the emotions that surround these decisions. Instead, find a way to get the decision discussed or reviewed openly. If you cannot accomplish this decision-review process and the apparently irrational decision stands, you may need to look for another job.

And here is the good lesson:

- Teams of very diverse people can work effectively to reach a common goal based on a shared work ethic and professional respect. If the team sees, understands and believes the vision around the business goal, great things can be accomplished.

Chapter 7: When Less (Mathematics) is More

Contributor: Director of Quantitative Data (DQD)

Narrator: *The Director of Quantitative Data (DQD) joined the Company early in its lifespan, immediately after finishing his Ph.D. He was bright, of course, and also inquisitive. He looked at the Company as an opportunity to create a system that would revolutionize the key decision-making process of the industry the Company served. He was intrigued that he would be instrumental in this effort and joined the Company ready to push the industry forward.*

I first became introduced to the Company and, through the Company to the dot.com revolution, during the final year of my Ph.D. Program at a Big 10 University. The Founder was interviewing our school as well as a competitive school to select one of us as technical advisors to the Company which, at that point, consisted only of the Founder and one assistant. The premise of the Company appeared to be a good one. The Founder wanted to provide the decision makers in the industry with statistically based recommendations for their critical decision-making process.

The goal of the Founder was to supplant the industry's current ad hoc decision-making method and elevate it to a higher, and, hopefully, if we got it right, more accurate level. The more exposed I became to the Founder's industry, the more dumbfounded I was with the low level of research and modeling these multimillion-dollar corporations engage in to make costly, key, decisions.

Well, as it turned out, our competitor was selected as the Company's technical advisors but this was not the last I heard from the Founder. In the summer after I had completed my Ph.D. I got a call. The Company had grown to five people and the Founder was looking for someone with a Ph.D. to serve as an in-house researcher and statistician. I soon found out that the importance of my Ph.D. had as much to do with the Company's need to tell prospective investors that it actually had a professional research staff as it did with research. The challenge of the assignment fascinated me and I accepted the job. Luckily, as it turned out for my productivity and sanity, I was able to operate from my home office in the Midwest.

My first visit to the Company's West Coast offices was eye opening and, in retrospect, indicative of how the dot.com explosion could only have occurred in that environment. Coming from my part of the Midwest where the sun virtually disappears for four straight months, the West Coast was a paradise. The naturally beautiful surrounding allows one to partially disengage from using logic. Feverish is the best way to describe the business climate at that time. Stories abounded of instant, enormous, personal wealth such as that of the infamous mailroom clerk at Cisco Systems who, through stock options and lucky timing, was a millionaire with a high school education. Everyone who had a tablespoon of ambition was fixated on the pursuit of the Holy Grail which was defined as getting stock options and taking the Company public. Long term meant next year and, as far as I could tell, there was little, if any, adult supervision on the entire West Coast.

The staff that the Founder had put together was experienced and seasoned. This was a marked departure from what I saw in other start-ups which were primarily run by kids. As a matter of fact, the venture capitalists (VCs) who came through the office when I was working in the West Coast office, seemed no more than twelve years old themselves. They often commented that they had rarely interviewed so much gray hair. We were a bona fide novelty. The venture capitalists seemed uncomfortable; had they no grandparents?

In addition to providing the stamp of research legitimacy, my future assignments with the Company included an exercise in futility, otherwise known as applying for a patent for our algorithms ("algorithm" is defined as a mathematical formula that solves a specific problem), and an exercise in creative writing, otherwise known as re-drafting the business plan. My first and primary assignment, however, was to work with the Founder, the VP and West Coast staff to create our "secret sauce". The Founder envisioned that our clients would input a bit of data about the critical decision into our software and our patent-still-pending algorithms would return an Index that enabled the customer to rank the proposed decision against their existing portfolio. This yet-to-be-developed Index was to be our secret sauce. Our Index would help the customer understand if the decision was likely to be profitable before his commitment. If our Index was "yes" then the decision would be a go. If the Index was "no" then the customer could try to re-negotiate the terms of the investment to get it to become profitable or could abandon it entirely. Very cool, if it could be done.

I first assembled an extensive database that I used to model and test the assumptions of our algorithms. Creating the secret sauce was a largely iterative process because we were testing an unproven, never-been-done-before vision. Over several months, we tested over and over until our Index reflected the real world fairly accurately. Believe it or not, at this point we were close to being the state of the art for research in our industry. One exceptional aspect of this work was that our products solved the investment decision question for our customers on-line and in real time. Suddenly, our clients with little or no research budget could access mathematical models and products grounded in statistics through technology that was affordable. Very cool stuff even for gray-hairs.

The level of statistics we employed was complex, and we became much more sophisticated than all but the largest research departments of our industry. In the early stages, the research went along smoothly. I conducted the analysis and the VP provided the industry experience to guide the process. We were making solid and exciting progress, secret sauce-wise. Enter the mercurial Chief Engineer.

The Chief Engineer ran the Information Technology (IT) group for the Company which was based in Utah, not in the West Coast office. Initially this was considered a managerial coup since locally based West Coast programmers were in high demand, unemployment was low, and West Coast salaries carried a huge housing premium. But locating the Chief Engineer and his team of engineers in Utah turned out to be a critical error for the Company. IT groups are difficult enough for any company to control since most managers really have no idea how their IT employees do what they do. Having an off-site IT group introduced another layer of difficulty.

Picture this combined with the general economic situation wherein engineers and programmers are in huge demand and feel themselves to be indispensable. Before long, it became apparent that the Company's Chief Engineer listened to no one, especially the people signing his paycheck. Now you've got the Company canoe leaving the dock in the middle of the night with no schedule, no destination, no stars or experience to guide it, and the Chief Engineer as captain, navigator, and most important passenger.

Not only did the Chief Engineer and his staff design our website without listening to our business-side staff, they meddled with the Index by raising its level of complexity. Given that none of the programmers or the Chief Engineer knew anything about the industry or business we were in, their meddling in this Company business decision was especially galling. The Chief Engineer's changes were done over the objections of the Company's experienced, seasoned, professionals. The Founder and the Chairman allowed the Chief Engineer's Index to be installed in our software over staff objections.

The ensuing year saw a battle between the two groups and the two competing indices. It goes without saying that the Chief Engineer prevailed since he knew that the Founder and the Chairman would not, could not, fire him. Oddly, it did not matter how many examples of inaccurate Indexing the VP showed the Founder or e-mailed to the Chief Engineer. The VP was ignored and the Index topic was closed according to the Founder and the Chairman. And, it did not matter even when the Founder gave a web-product sales demonstration and the prospective customer pointed out the inaccuracy of the Index. The Index topic was still closed. The situation deteriorated to the point that the Chief Engineer's Index was used in the software application while our consultants quietly used my original one for their clients.

In addition to our in-house issues, it wasn't until after being with the Company a full year that I understood how the deck was stacked against software start-up companies by the venture capital

(VC) community. Software companies that produced only moderate revenue growth and had solid products were of no value to the VCs. What mattered at this time was that the investors got a quick, positive financial return and got in and out of young companies as swiftly as possible.

Here is how their Return-On-Investment math worked. When raising money to invest in companies such as ours, the venture capitalists had to promise high returns to their own investors since they were competing against other less risky capital sectors for the investor's money. These high, promised, returns then forced the VCs to bet on long shots since only these could theoretically generate the high returns required. The VCs hunted for the "Killer Software Application."

The Killer App was defined as the software package that would become industry-dominant for that particular use, as Quick Books is to small business accounting or Word is to word processing. The Company never had the time to unseat the traditional methods of research in our industry to become the industry standard or the Killer App for our business.

The VCs did not want to hear that we were revolutionizing a stodgy industry which would, unfortunately, take some time. They needed good financial results fast. As my second year with the Company unfolded it became apparent that software companies whose products weren't fully embraced by their market were not going to be able to make it through second funding rounds. The liquidity in the market had left and was not to return for several years.

I left the Company that summer after nearly two years because, as I explained to people, I was due back on Planet Earth. Although my stock options are worthless, I look back at my experience with the Company as a fairly positive one; for a brief period, we were state of the art in research for our huge industry.

There are important lessons to take away from these two years:

- Even a strict reliance on high level mathematics should incorporate the messiness that is often involved in real life. Sometimes less math is more.

- Senior management should never accept egregious employee actions. It is not in any company's best interest for technologists to override business experts.

- Understand your product's life cycle and how quickly you will be able to switch customers to your new way of doing things. If it is going to take time, and an aggressive sales force, to get market share for your product then match the patience of your investors to your product life cycle.

Inventing a secret sauce that works is very cool stuff!

Chapter 8: "Customer Service – How May I Help You?"

Contributor: The Company's Customer Service Representative

Narrator: The Customer Service Representative (CSR) was smart, cheerful and had a great sense of humor. He worked with everyone in the Company to learn the software that was being developed so he could train customers and answer their questions. He developed good relationships with important customers because they learned they could depend on him. He gave willingly of his time and energy and established a high standard of customer service for the growing Company, yet the Founder and the Chairman never understood his value to the Company.

The stock options the Company offered me were the fulfillment of an elusive fantasy that I had read about and was greatly intrigued with. At the time that I joined the Company magazines, such as *Wired* and *Fast Company*, and all of the newspapers were running stories about the seemingly effortless wealth that was generated for average employees who had stock options in high-tech companies. Prior to joining the Company, I worked for a real estate title and escrow business and there was no chance of stock options in that line of work, but I had friends who had stock options from their companies, and I was envious. When my interview with the Company included a discussion of my stock options, I was thrilled! For the first time since moving to a very expensive part of the West Coast, I had the prospect of not only being able to survive but also to thrive. Those stock options gave me the hope of buying my own piece of residential real estate and finally getting a feeling of personal economic security.

I was hired as the Customer Service Representative (CSR) for the Company when the firm was about twenty months old. In earlier jobs, I had been a CSR for over eight years, and I had a high level of comfort working with customers over the phone and live on the computer. In several of my earlier CSR jobs, I had been instructed to use standard customer service scripts. In effect, I listened to the customer's complaint and responded using a prepared script that appeared on my computer monitor. You barely listened to the customer and had to stick to the most appropriate canned speech. If you have ever received unsatisfactory customer service from a 1-800 phone number, prepared scripts are why. That rep does not really listen to you, as you have long suspected, but they must mollify you and then mollify the next cranky customer. Scripts allow the company to "control the message and insure that each customer receives the same high level of customer service."

The Company, however, planned to subscribe to a new Sales and CSR software that enabled our prospects and clients to sit in their office and see my computer screen on *their* computer screen, so I could train them as well as spontaneously answer their questions. The Company didn't know about canned scripts, and I wasn't going to tell them because nothing is worse for the customer. I mean, CSR notes and training are great, but people want to have real conversations with real humans when they have a question or a problem. I was eager to use this new software and add it to my skill set, and, believe me, those stock options had worked on me like the red cape works on bulls in Spain!! Ole!

I was hired when the Company was in the final stages of preparing the web-based tools for the initial product launch at their national convention. These were very exciting days as there were marketing meetings, advertising meetings, product development meetings and I, as the only CSR, was included in many of them. For the first time in my professional life I actually sat at the conference table with the Founder, CTO2, and the VP of the company I was working for. At this time, a high value was placed on everyone's input and opinions, and I found it invigorating, nerve-racking, and exciting all at once! I was happy with my job for the first time in years. I was finally a part of a real team in the true sense of the word! I had never worked in a company where we all high-fived each other over the smallest victory. This environment was all so new to me and I loved it!

Here is, briefly, one of my best memories of those early days. It was decided that due to our remote offices, we, as a Company, needed a bonding experience and it turned into an amazing evening! Our technology team and their families were flown in to the West Coast headquarters from Utah, as was our Director of Data and his wife from Chicago, for a night of bowling and then wonderful food. The Company arranged for a bus so we could be together, drink, and get home safely. We piled in, and what an assortment – West Coast employees, plus Chicago and Utah, plus wives and kids – it was fantastic. We were driven into the city and had cocktails on the bus and cocktails during the bowling. We all let our hair down and had a hundred laughs. The VP taught our Russian female programmer how to bowl, and we got hysterical when she got a strike. It was a fabulous time!

After bowling, the bus took us all to a very cool part of the city and to a wonderful restaurant. Then, the Founder and the Chairman and his wife joined us for dinner. The food was excellent and we had more cocktails. Amazingly, I even remember the bus ride back to the office, but I was definitely feeling no pain, honey-child!! I had so much fun that night – all I could think was that I had finally made it. I was really a dot-comer and I was going to be a dot-survivor – with fabulous stock options.

Now, back to work. We had two kinds of customers in those days, paying customers and non-paying beta test customers. The beta test customers were testing our web-based products for free and we hoped to convert them into real, paying customers.

Beta test is software jargon for letting your most desired customers use your product for, say, two weeks for free. These prospective customers got a sneak preview of our new product, which the customers all felt was very cool. The VP and I would do the initial training to give the beta testers access and training on our system. We would then follow up in about ten days to get their comments on our new products and web-site and try to hook them as real customers. I posted the notes from these feedback phone calls on a big board so everyone in the Company could read the good, bad, or indifferent comments of the beta testers. Each of us then thought about ways to change our products to eliminate any bad commentary. It was like being in a supersonic jet!! The beta test customers were seeing how a web-based technology could be used to get key information instantly with the click of a button. Normally they would have to order this information and wait for several days to get the data. Every time we introduced a new beta tester to our products, their input was very positive overall. The positive comments energized us about the future of our small company!

We also had real, paying customers – people that had been beta testers, and whom we had been able to convert to paying our annual subscription fee for unlimited use of our web-based tools. We were able to convert slightly over half of our beta testers to paying customers, and we saw this as the path of success for the Company. My job with these customers was to train the folks who were going to actually use our web software on a daily basis. Thank goodness our system was easy to use!

In those early days I wore many hats. I worked with the beta testers and the subscribing customers to ease them into our new world of products. I gave sales demonstrations with the VP at 7:00am to accommodate the East Coast prospects. I wrote the Company's User's Guide, and I am still so proud of the accomplishment that I want to tell you about it.

We needed a tool which could be e-mailed to our new customers and would be easy for them to use as a reference document on how to get the most out of our on-line web products. I had a meeting with my manager and the VP to discuss the User's Guide. We decided that we wanted to make a change from the 300-page, tiny type, incorrect user's manuals that accompanied many software packages. I was charged to write a brief, accurate, e-mailable User's Guide for our technology challenged customers. My User's Guide was 15 pages long, and I figured out how to incorporate screen shots from our actual web-site into the document so the image on your computer screen was the same as in the Guide. It was very practical and cool and the customers loved it, which is one reason I am so proud of it. But the second reason is that the VP continued to send it to customers for two years after I was laid off from the Company.

I hope you are wondering, laid off?? Lordy, yes, I was laid off.

Shortly after our second successful beta-test period the Chairman became more involved with the Company. Both of our beta tests had high tester-to-customer conversion rates but the Company's sales strategy after these two efforts was loosey-goosey. The Founder and the Chairman decided that everyone needed to change hats, and we were pulled from our departments to help with sales. I was told to cold-call prospects and set up sales demonstrations for sales staff. This was not my forte, and like others within the Company, I tried to give it my best effort. I won't say that I was a failure...

Then the Founder and the Chairman decided that we would sponsor a Treasure Hunt on our website to get prospective customers to sign-in and "take our website for a test drive." We had many meetings and discussions about how to create a Treasure Hunt that would result in the prospective customer taking a complete tour of our web-based products before finding the Treasure. The Founder and the Chairman insisted that the Treasure should not be easy to find and we should make the hunters wander through our entire web site. When the prospective customer found the Treasure, they would then be entered into a lottery for a Grand Prize. Many of us disagreed with the wandering-through-the-whole-site and highest-level-of-difficulty thing and suggested easier alternatives. No one, we argued, has that much time or patience. Wasn't this supposed to be even a little bit of fun for the hunters? Anyhoo, the Founder and the Chairman prevailed and a mailing went out to hundreds of prospective clients announcing the Treasure Hunt and the contest for the Grand Prize.

I was told to be in the office at 6:00am on the Monday morning after the Treasure Hunt mailing, to personally answer the phones and field questions about the web site. The VP joined me at 7:00am just in case I needed a backup. We had time on our hands as there were no phone calls, so I tried to follow the instructions to find the Treasure that had been hidden into our software over the weekend. No one in the Company knew the web-site as well as the VP and I – neither of us could find the Treasure. How were the customers going to? No Grand Prize was given away, so at least the Company did not spend that money.

Well, the Company had seventy-eight client companies on our roster, and then we hit a financial brick wall. The Founder struggled to re-define our business plan on what seemed like a daily basis. Could we ever go public? Would my stock options ever come to fruition? Was I doomed to paying a fortune in rent for a tiny, noisy, studio apartment for the rest of my life?

All of a sudden, the Founder and the Chairman perceived me as "overhead", which was not strictly the truth if you consider all the tester-to-customer conversions I took part in. The Founder and the Chairman were looking for reasons why sales had stalled and for ways to cut expenses. So, even though I had managed to create and maintain good customer relationships and was on a first name basis with many important customers, this was not seen as "sales" and I was indeed, laid off. So here are the high-tech lessons I have for you:

• Very different people can pull together successfully for a common cause. I will always remember the Company roller coaster ride, the ups and downs and the corners that we took at 70 mph without hesitation. We may not have succeeded as a Company but we all wanted to.

• Changing the Company sales strategy on a weekly basis may mean there is no Company sales strategy. If you are in senior management, you need to think about this and get the resources you need to get out of neutral gear.

• For the first five months of my employment with the Company the employees were treated as equals. All of us, regardless of title, were able to give opinions and advice based on earlier professional experiences, and these contributions were welcomed and considered. This was a heady experience for many of us, and I loved it. Then we got a new layer of people who, oddly enough, had little experience doing what we were doing. It was these inexperienced folks who made a series of decisions, such as the infamous Treasure Hunt. Those of us with expertise were shunted aside, and I believe, we became invisible. This turned out, in my view, to be the negative turning point for the Company.

But I will always remember the fun we had. I had more laughs at the Company in the ten months that I was there than I did in my five prior years with big corporations. The friendships I formed at the Company in that brief time have lasted – our friendships went beyond our cubicles and have colored my life in a very positive way. We accomplished a lot but had fun, too. And my User's Guide was used for two and a half years!

Chapter 9: The Price Was Never Right

Contributor: The First Salesman

> **Narrator**: *The First Salesman started with the Company in Product Development and after a year he moved to Sales when the second suite of products was launched. It was then that the Founder realized that the Company had no sales team. The First Salesman was an outgoing, high energy, bright, extroverted fellow who was a natural team player and he should have excelled on a sales team. However, the lack of any sales force training or support such as cold calling assistance and infrastructure such as a company brochure, minimized his success from the start. This pushed the First Salesman over the edge in six months flat.*

I was fresh from a job in the public sector where every project had two, three, maybe four constituencies that had to be considered, met with, debated with, and dealt with before any decision could be made by my boss. Consequently, I worked very hard but little ever got done. I was drawn to the Company because, in contrast, the Company's industry was famous for hammering out deals and at the end of the day you either closed the deal or you didn't. The very nature of the industry was that things got done and after a few years in the public sector I was eager for that environment. For a guy like me with a degree in city planning, or the study of urban process rather than urban progress, this seemed very exciting.

I started at the Company in Product Development. For the first ten months of my employment I helped develop the web-based products for the Company. Report after report, map after map were specifically developed to be a concise snap-shot of the information that every one of our future customers was going to need to make a frequent, industry, business decision. For the first time in my career, I was building tools that would facilitate rather than avoid making business decisions.

Since the Company's office was an open warehouse with carpet (very cool, or at least we were supposed to think) there was no place to have a private conversation. When something needed to be discussed quietly, you and your supervisor went for a walk to the local delicatessen, which was across the parking lot. One day the VP asked me to walk over to the deli with her. It turned out that the Founder finally realized that we were about to roll out the second suite of our products, and there was no sales force. Up until that time, our sales process consisted of getting potential customers to test our products for a two-week period; after that we tried to convert them to becoming paid annual subscribers. We had been very good at converting testers into customers, and this success disguised the fact that we had no sales team. We were all hoping that the launch of this second set of products was going to be so successful that we were going to be flooded with sales calls and we would need people who were ready to sell the product. The VP wanted to know if I was interested in moving to Sales. There was the possibility of getting commissions and, frankly, it was something I always wanted to try and had mentioned in my original interview. I made the move to Sales with hopeful ambitions.

My first problem was with product pricing. This gets complicated but hang in there with me. The Company had originally rolled out a package of various data-based reports as their initial suite of products. The second suite of products was going to be a package of assorted maps that would work with the reports. Many customers did not need, or want, all of the maps and all of the reports. So, as we got closer to this second product roll out, we had to develop packages that mixed reports and maps in combinations and at prices that made sense for our range of clients. This was a complex, three-dimensional-matrix process because at the time there were several ways to obtain our products:

- They could be purchased over the Internet with a credit card (we were having trouble with the installation of the credit card user interface on our web site but we had to get going and did not let this stop us!) To add to this confusion, the Founder wanted us to have one set price if the customers ran the report themselves and a second price if we ran the report for the customer and then e-mailed it to them.

- Annual subscriptions could be obtained for a set number of users per client. This subscription pricing depended on the number of users the client wanted to have on our system, the products the client wanted to subscribe to and how big the client's business was.

- Or the customer could buy a one-time package of products for a fixed fee.

The combinations were complicated because the Founder liked to be able to negotiate freely with customers, but since I was moving to Sales I needed a simple price sheet, so I volunteered to take on this mix and match variable-pricing task.

One Saturday (it was hockey season and the Boston Bruins were on a rare roll just to put my sacrifice into perspective for you) the VP and I sat down to put all the pricing together for individual reports and the subscription packages. Fortunately, before I joined the Company, I had purchased a somewhat similar product for my former employer. This enabled me to know the price of data and which software was required to extract the meaningful information. In addition, our high school Intern had also done a fairly exhaustive study of our competition and had cataloged all of their prices. The VP and I felt that it was appropriate for the two of us to do the pricing matrix because, with the CSR, we were the main people who spoke with and worked with our testers and early customers. We heard clearly what they wanted and what they would pay for our products. In short, we were fully prepared for this task and we developed packages that, we felt, positioned us appropriately in the marketplace.

We were wrong.

On Monday morning we met at our big conference table and presented our pricing schedule to the Founder, the Chairman, and an outside consultant/investor. Neither the Chairman nor the consultant/investor had ever worked in our industry, but they argued that the VP and I had grossly undervalued our products. Their argument was that the products were "hugely valuable," and the price for the annual subscriptions, for example, should be ten times what we were suggesting.

We persisted that we would need to be price competitive at first to gain market share, which we had little of at that time, and to get customers in the door. We also said that in subsequent years we would be able to raise subscription prices when the customers had successfully used our products and could see for themselves how "hugely valuable" they were. Nevertheless, we were told to aggressively re-work our pricing sheet.

There were several more of these pricing meetings and the Founder, the Chairman and the consultant/investor never wavered from their position that they knew better than we did what the true value of our products were. I wondered if I had somehow slipped back into the public-sector world of endless debate and discussion by opinionated yet unknowledgeable people.

Eventually a pricing sheet was finalized – too high, if you ask me – and it was time to move onto the proverbial sales "message." This proved to be my second problem area. I voted for a direct pitch that would clearly spell out what our Company did and why using our web-based products was a smart step into the future for our customers. The Founder and the Chairman voted for obfuscation because they did not want to be lumped with our competitors. I was told to begin my sales calls with a vague, meaningless opening such as, "We provide intelligent tools to help you make better business decisions." Well, who doesn't? And what does that really mean anyway?

The un-debatable fact was that data was at the heart of our products. In creating the message for my cold calls, however, the directive from the Founder and the Chairman was that I was to differentiate the Company from other data providers by not calling our products data driven.

My cold calls went something like this.

"Hi, I'm the First Salesman and my Company provides intelligent tools to help you make better business decisions"

Prospective customer: Silence.

Me, following up on the silence: "My Company has a proprietary system that will dramatically reduce the guesswork inherent in most business expansion decisions."

Prospective customer: "Whose data do you use?"

Me, again: "We are more than just data. Our products have a matching index that allows you to see instantly over the Internet if there are enough of your type of customers in a market for you to be successful."

Prospective customer: "But whose data do you use?"

Me: "We can match your prospective markets to your existing markets and give you the answer over the Internet." I would then plead, "Don't you see how this could be useful for your business?"

Prospective customer: "Well". And then he would thank me for my time and hang up.

The not-selling of data got very difficult. It became almost a joke with me that when the Founder walked by my cubicle I wouldn't use the "D" word, but as soon as the Founder was out of earshot, you could hear me in hushed, desperation whisper over the phone, "Yes, we use XYZ's data. It is the best that money can buy and we have rock bottom prices..."

My third problem area was the endless negotiation at the Company. As I mentioned before, our Company was in an ancient industry that required an ancient skill: negotiation. As the only salesman, I was required to sell our products, that is, to negotiate with our industry's professional, hard-core brokers. These guys were tough, tough negotiators who consistently beat me up on price, when I even got that far in the sales process with them.

Then I would have to take the proposal, with my blood all over it, to the Founder for approval. I always had to renegotiate the deal with the Founder. When the Founder was finished negotiating with our prospective client through me, I would then have to loop back to the prospective client and start just about at the beginning. I felt like a hockey puck in a playoff game that had just gone into sudden death overtime.

Things became increasingly frustrating. As an example, here is the story of the most amazing business meeting I have ever attended – and keep in mind I used to work in the public sector so that is saying something. The meeting, also attended by the Founder and the Chairman, was with a prestigious investment bank – our biggest investor in the Company – in which some of the luminaries from the investment bank decided to have a conversation with me about our current sales procedures. In essence, they wanted to know how I was tracking my progress with cold calls, developing leads and following up. I described our process to date and how, when we began, I had estimated that I would be able to sell a subscription to about one in twenty contacts. After a few months of testing this theory, it was turning out to be true. "Well then, you need to make about ten calls a day, to hit your sales goal." I had to give the investment banker credit; he was good with the numbers.

But then our investment banker went on. "You know at our firm, we know Sales inside and out. For us, it is a well-oiled machine. We have rigorous tests that we use to assess an individual's ability to sell, and we provide constructive feedback on an individual's sales technique."

"Really" I said, "you give assessment, training, and support to your sales force? Is there any way you could give me the same sales assessment, training and support? After all, I need help and you are a major investor in our Company."

He replied, "No."

"Why not?"

"It's proprietary and we can't share that with you," he said.

In a sense, help was available yet unavailable. The message was clear, our largest investor could have helped us with our sales technique, but instead he seemed willing to see us wallow in our own frustration, fear of failure, and piss away his bank's investment. Dammit, and thanks for your support, Mr. Investment Banker! Here are the lessons I learned with the Company:

- **Know the marketplace before you enter it.** Our 16-year-old high school Intern did enough research on the web in a month to understand how our products should be priced. Yet the Founder, the Chairman, and the consultant/investor who knew nothing won the pricing argument. Come on!

- **Train your sales staff before sending them out onto a professional negotiator's turf.** Having untrained staff try to do phone sales to professional negotiators is a waste of time, and it annoys potential clients. Perhaps, in our situation, if we had lower, more competitive prices to begin with we would have had fewer pricing discussions with our customers. Oh well, too late.

- **Don't undermine your Sales force.** Don't renegotiate every deal your sales team brings you. Sales people should be focused on negotiating with the outside world and not with the Company they work for.

Chapter 10: Guru Guidance

Contributor: The Executive Vice President

Narrator: *The Executive Vice President of Sales and Marketing (EVP) came to the Company with a big smile, a booming voice and a larger-than-life personality. Just as important, he brought his personal, career-long relationships with the movers and shakers in the Founder's industry. He was going to be instrumental in getting the savviest businesses in the industry to become customers of the Company and he was exactly what the Company needed. The EVP was an industry guru and he was going to save the day.*

Well, once upon a time, I was the President of a mid-size, successful company, and the Founder actually reported to me. Then I sold the business, made a fair amount of money for a lot of my employees, and retired ahead of schedule. The Founder contacted me out of the blue and wanted to talk with me. It was very mysterious and of course, I was curious. "What's up, kid?" I asked. The Founder and the Chairman had a proposition for me. This could be interesting, very interesting!

I bought them breakfast. The Founder brought the same great smile and the same high energy, which I knew could often result in chaos, to our breakfast. Turned out, the Founder and the Chairman wanted me, with my high-level industry contacts, to come and work three days a week for the Company. I was offered a title, Vice President of Sales and Marketing, a base salary, and a commission structure that I did not need but would take because of the principal of the thing. I was hesitant at our breakfast, because in the past, it had not always been simple to work with the Founder due to the chaos thing. But retirement was just not my gig. I am an energetic, optimistic, enthusiastic deal-maker, and it did sound like they needed help at a level I could provide. I asked to meet some of the other key people before I decided and was told "Sure."

A couple of days after our breakfast, I rode my bike over to the office to meet CTO2 and the VP, as they were senior employees and we would be working together closely. They both seemed nice, if a bit too intense and too tightly wrapped for me. I believe in work hard/play hard and make life fun. Apparently, they both worked hard – maybe too hard. But then they gave me the insider's tour of the web-based software that they were building for the Founder. The VP gave the web product demonstration and CTO2 pitched in as needed. When they showed me the products they were working on, I understood their intensity. Our industry had nothing like what they were doing. The products they showed me were five steps ahead of what I knew was available, the ease of use was brilliant, and the speed at which data could be retrieved and the accuracy of the end products just blew me away. These were products that I knew could revolutionize our traditional industry. For the first time, I thought that it might very well be possible for the Founder to realize the dream of becoming the new Industry Standard with these people and the work they were doing. I have always said that my talent for making money stems from the fact that I am an unapologetic opportunist. And this was a heck of an opportunity.

There was just one hitch. What they showed me were in-house, live products that could only be accessed by a maximum of two computers in the West Coast office and the computers of the five software engineers in the Utah office. These products were rough and not ready for prime time. They had not been fully tested in-house, let alone by the outside world. This meant that there was no way for me to demonstrate these products, so how was I ever going to sell them? "How about a PowerPoint slide show using a mock-up of the web products," the VP asked. How lame is that, I thought.

"When will the software be ready to access live, so I can show folks the real deal?" I asked.

"In time for our huge, industry convention," the Founder replied.

"Three months away?? Wow! And great," I replied.

I noticed the VP and CTO2 both looked at their watches. They got back to work while the Founder and I talked this over.

What an opportunity! The Founder and I negotiated 2.5 days of my time each week for the original salary that had been offered to me. (You should remember not to negotiate with a negotiator!) And I had to insist on Executive Vice President, rather than the VP title, but as that cost the company nothing the Founder was agreeable.

In the end, I did use the (lame) PowerPoint presentation as a means of seducing potential customers into making appointments with us at our convention so they could finally see the Founder's miracle "live." I spent my 2.5 days per week on the phone, pitching everyone I knew and calling in a lot of my life-long industry chips. This was me at my very best! Most people in our industry like me and I like them and there I was, feet on my desk, on the speaker phone, renewing old acquaintances, and wowing people with the very cool thing I was working on. Bye-bye retirement!

The meeting list for our convention grew quickly. A cutting-edge, home furnishings retailer was interested, as was a start-up, hyper cool, new Zen/breathe/love tea shop chain. The best, upscale, national jewelry store wanted a private look at what we could do. So did a fast-growth retailer who sold personalized kid's toys. A French bath and body shop retailer wanted a peek, so did an exclusive handbag company and a hip doughnut chain (yes, there is such a thing). I lined them up and was amazed at the wide assortment of interested companies. Be it high-end, low-end, or moderate-priced merchandise or be it for adults, teens, or kids – all of the best and the brightest companies were keenly interested in seeing this new idea. From my point of view, there were only two challenges left. First, get the pricing right for our products. Second, close the brand-name deals first, and the rest of the companies would follow. These were not insignificant challenges.

The First Salesman had shared with me some of the internal difficulties that he had getting the Founder and the Chairman to agree on pricing. I had a theory that said make the price on a new way of doing something not an issue in the sales process. In other words, don't add the risk of a high price to the risk of a new technology. This is common sense, right? Also, I thought it made sense for us to have an affordable price to limit the number of people in each prospective company who had to sign off on our purchase order. Everyone inside a company who has to sign off on any high cost purchase feels that they are entitled to an opinion and you, the salesman, want to streamline the sales process and shut the door on objections. Simple was the right way to get brand-name customers quickly and easily and build market share momentum. I had lunch with the Founder to discuss the price issue outside of the office. I believed my older, grayer head and experience would prevail.

Don't misunderstand me, the Founder was smart, but could not see the forest for the trees on this pricing issue. A lot of time and money had been spent to develop these new products and the Founder wanted big ticket customers ASAP. This is not the way to go, I argued. Get the important clients and their word-of-mouth-advertising. Then, when they are addicted to your products and cannot even imagine how they ran their business without your services, raise your price steadily and relentlessly. I got nowhere with my line of reasoning with the Founder, so to give myself some wiggle room, I told everyone with whom I had made a convention appointment that we were still working on our pricing. Reason, I believed, would win at the end of the day.

We gave a ton of product demonstrations at the convention and really got the buzz going. Things were sizzling and the official launch of the web-based products was right on the horizon.

But there were some internal, personnel, issues that blew up right before the convention and, then again, right before the product launch. These had nothing to do with me but the problems were fairly substantial and involved the VP, CTO2, and the Chief Engineer in the Utah office. I am a real people-person, but even I had experienced how hard it can be work with key people in remote offices when I was President of my own company. I know that communication by conference call alone is difficult. Nuances can easily get lost, in particular if the people doing the talking do not know each other well. To make a long story short, the technology guys were beating up on the business people and I intuitively knew that this was wrong. I bought the Founder a Manhattan one evening.

It should be no surprise to you when I say I am a direct communicator and a straight shooter. I hated dealing with personnel "issues" when I was President of my former company, and so I had a Human Resource (HR) person who handled all of it for me, except for the most extreme crap. My HR gal extorted a lot of money from my company but she was worth every penny, as far as I was concerned.

I could see that the Founder was trying to spin too many plates at one time. Many founders have little experience dealing with bright, proud, experienced professionals who are banging heads. The Company was on the brink of success – the convention was great, the products were fantastic, and the list of likely customers was terrific – and I did not want to see all that effort blow-up. Over the second Manhattan, I leveled with the Founder and I said that for the long-term good of the Company, an operations professional should be hired and that the three head-butting employees should report to this person who would take this basically crippling situation off the Founder's plate.

The Founder stared at me.

"Look," I said, "You don't have time to deal with this crap, but someone needs to or all your star performers are going to walk."

I pressed home my point by then saying, "The blunt truth is that you and the Company need a COO. I am not betraying you nor am I criticizing your management skills or style but I see a problem and it looks serious to me.

"But *I* am the CEO and the COO," the Founder replied.

I looked at the Founder in disbelief – the company's star performers were not being effectively managed. I asked for the check, we jousted over who was going to pay for the drinks but I prevailed and we left.

My thoughts? Well, it was the Founder's company. I suppose I may have spoken out of turn, and that I had caused hurt feelings. But I had only told the business-truth. No one person has the skills to do every job in the company, so it's better to find out what your strengths are and focus your work efforts in those areas. This is the way I see things.

A few weeks later, the Founder offered to buy me coffee and said the Company had cash flow problems and would I mind working on commission only? I did mind. Two weeks later I left the Company to travel with my great wife.

Lessons? Don't buy your boss manhattans. And don't let the Founder buy you coffee.

Chapter 11: The Dearth of a Salesman

Contributor: The Director of Sales

Narrator: *Our second salesman was hired with the understanding that he would be made the Director of Sales. He had been a top sales producer for another company that sold web-based services and the Founder and the Chairman thought it would be a natural transition for him to sell web-based services to our market even though he had no contacts or experience in our industry. He found the deck stacked against him from the very first week he was on the job. Then he started his second week with the Company and his situation got dramatically worse.*

Just eight days ago I started with the Company and left my old job where I had an office, small, but an office, and a sales team of nine people to work with, bounce ideas around with and relax with in the early evening. My previous company had corporate marketing materials, of course, and a price sheet that covered any combination of things a customer might want to buy from us. There also was a four-person support staff that made cold-calls and pre-qualified sales leads for us, the salespeople. The serious down side of my former job was that my boss, the Head of Sales, (HoS, as I called her) was right across the hall and I chafed at that. She was constantly tracking every move we made so that I felt, as did the other sales people, that we were constantly being supervised. When the Founder offered me a higher base salary and the opportunity to be the Director of Sales and leave the HoS behind, I snapped it up.

So now, here I was beginning my second week with the Company and I had the suspicion that I had made a CLM – a Career Limiting Mistake. I had no office, a two-person sales team, no camaraderie to speak of, certainly no corporate marketing materials, no price sheet that anyone could agree on, and not a support staff cold-caller in sight. And to top it all off, I was responsible, as the Director of Sales, for producing sales!! But at least my new boss, the Executive Vice President of Sales and Marketing (EVP), was a great guy and not a "Boss" like HoS had been. The EVP had been in the industry for 35 years and he knew everyone. He was going to introduce the First Salesman and me to his industry contacts and help us approach, pitch, and close our first customers. He was the only lifeline that I could see for getting around the self-inflicted wounds that existed in the "Sales Department" at the Company and because he appeared to like me, I could sleep at night.

On this, my second Monday morning with the Company, I ran up the stairs to the office, a bit late because I had hit the surf at

Ocean Beach a half hour late this morning. (I should tell you that I am a serious recreational surfer and on my first trip to the west coast from the Midwest, I fell in love with the Pacific Ocean. There is something about the irony of riding a violent, powerful, angry, wave in the "pacific" ocean that I love. Totally. Oh yes, I can do surfer speak but I was an English major in college, and I respect the language. Totally. Don't worry, I will not "Gnarly, dude!" you to death.) The Founder and the EVP were in a low-voiced conversation at the Founder's desk. My first thought was that they were laying out the sales targets for the coming week and so I headed over to my workstation to open up my computer. The First Salesman, a nice guy and about my age, was there ahead of me and we casually exchanged notes about our weekend. He was married with one child and a pregnant wife – I am single and have a girlfriend. No kidding, I had had the better weekend by a long shot.

At the time I joined the Company the first set of web-based products had been beta tested and released to the Company's client base and the second set of products was just finishing the beta test process and was poised to be released today to the clients. It was pretty exciting. The Company had figured out that if you ask potential customers to test the web-based products for free, customers love that "sneak preview" and can actually get a bit addicted to the products. So great, all I had to do was close the sales to the beta customers and my commission was good for the short term. The long term, with no support staff, contacts, or marketing materials scared the daylights out of me, but I knew I had the EVP to lean on when the long term showed up.

I heard the Founder and the EVP head down the stairs and leave the building. I turned to the First Salesman and asked if he knew what was happening, but he just shook his head and said they were likely going to the deli across the parking lot for some privacy. Whatever, I thought.

Thirty minutes later the Founder returned to the office alone. The First Salesman and I were called into the Founder's office area because there evidently was something for us to discuss. I was tense and didn't want it to show so I slouched in the chair with my legs stretched straight out before me, stared at my knees, and tried to look bored. In order to save the Company some money, the Founder said, the EVP had agreed to become a consultant on an as-needed basis. My head snapped up and I stared at the Founder. I took my glasses off and cleaned them as a stall tactic to ward off the panic curling in me. The Founder went on to say that between the two of them they had so many overlapping industry contacts that the Company did not anticipate using the EVP much in the future. In fact, the Founder was taking the Sales function back and, starting immediately, the three of us would be working closely together from here on out. I was as stunned as the First Salesman, only I hid it better.

The Founder continued that we would begin having sales meetings on Monday mornings at 10:00am and Thursday afternoons at 3:00pm every week. The Founder was going to run the meetings and we were to assume that the meetings wouldn't last more than an hour and a half. We were to bring our sales leads to the meetings, our sales pipeline reports to the meetings, our phone logs and the list of product demonstrations we, with the VP, had given to potential customers. I hope I did not look as freaked as I was. Maybe my old company would take me back?

The Founder then hit the intercom button on the office phone and told the VP, whose work station was thirty feet away, to join us. I took a deep breath and tried to figure out *why* what had just happened had happened. When the Founder reiterated the EVP story, the VP turned white and then red.

VP: "You fired the EVP?"

Founder: "Oh no, he will become a consultant to the Company. You know how tight cash is."

VP: "But didn't you just say that we were not going to be using him?"

Founder: "I have many of the same contacts he does – so we won't need him."

VP: "Today is, in many respects, the day we have all been working toward for eighteen months. We, in Product Development, and the programmers are now ready to hand the first two suites of products over to the Sales staff and you are telling us our senior sales guy, our EVP, our ace in the hole who knew everyone in our industry, is gone. With all due respect, our Sales staff consists of the First Salesman who good-naturedly came to Sales from Product Development but has no industry contacts. The new guy, Director of Sales, is not fully trained on the web-based products, has no industry contacts and this is only his eighth day with the Company. And today we are passing the baton to our Sales force??"

(The VP was frazzled and looked like hell because she had been in the office six hours on Saturday and four on Sunday so I excused her statement-of-the-obvious as just a female, emotional outburst. Probably hormonal.)

The Founder looked a bit startled that the VP hadn't thought it was a great day to ditch the EVP.

"I told you," the Founder said, "I have many of the same contacts that the EVP did and we will be just fine. We need to save cash and reducing the EVP's time was the common-sense thing to do."

At this point the Founder head for the shower and we were told to go hit the phones and "make it happen." All I could think was, "Oh, my God, I am in such deep trouble." No EVP, no contacts, no cold-calling support staff, no support materials and a ticked off VP. Well, I thought, it couldn't get any worse – but it did.

When the Founder had come out of the shower and was dressed, I was called on the intercom and told that the First Salesman and I should meet for our now standard Monday sales meeting. Two hours later we dragged ourselves, completely shredded, back to our workstations. Of course, we now had only three working days until our Thursday sales meeting, so we hit the phones to get strangers interested in talking with us. It would have been hard enough with the EVP's contacts, but without those golden introductions it was beyond bleak. But I had "committed to the wave" and now had to ride it out.

Was it remotely possible that the Founder didn't know that, to be done correctly, Sales must be a discipline? HoS, at my former job, was constantly after all of us to identify our target customers, approach them, pitch them, and follow-up, follow-up, follow-up. In my former job, HoS had preached follow-up until she made you crazy. HoS drilled into us that we had a high-tech product to sell to low-tech people. In that job, HoS made us actually memorize the benefits of our products, which stifled my spontaneity, as well as our advantages over our competitors. She once went too far and taped the "Benefits and Competitive Advantages" to each of our computers. Come on, now. I certainly do not advocate anything as formal as the system HoS had in place because it crushed my creativity, but on the other hand I loved my bonus checks.

Like that former job, the Founder's Company was trying to sell a new product, using a new technology and most of the executives in this, my new industry, lived in caves. In fact, the Founder was not even a computer whiz and should have known that to get our industry to embrace this new idea was going to take contacts, hand holding, and time.

But what about all of the Founder's industry contacts, you are thinking. Well, that was strange, too. The Founder used those contacts but did not share those contacts. From time to time I was allowed to sit in on a sales call with the Founder but was never handed a list of companies and contact names and told to go for it. It was almost as though both of us, the First Salesman and I, were in competition with the Founder for bagging the most customers. Like I said, it was weird.

We bumbled along like this for a couple of months. The VP and the Customer Service Representative (CSR) helped out and converted a lot of the beta testers to customers so we did have some sales on my watch. But the Founder got increasingly anxious and our twice-a-week Sales meetings turned into relentless inquisitions. I began to hate Monday and Thursday, which, of course, ruined my Sundays and Wednesdays.

As the Founder got more and more desperate, the sales team was transformed into the enemy. The message which was wordlessly conveyed to me was that if it were not for the First Salesman and me, the Company would be successful. The Founder hit the intercom or popped unannounced into our workspace about fifty times a day to see who we were on the phone with. It got so obnoxious that I brought an inexpensive web camera into the office, set it up under my workstation and aimed it in the direction of the Founder's office area so that I could have some advanced warning on my computer screen if the Founder approached. In surfer's terms, I was watching "the local demon drop in" but the First Salesman thanked me for my surveillance efforts.

Little of what went on in the office made good common sense to me. We did not have the tools to do the job and yet when any of us made a stab at developing a price sheet, a marketing piece or a sales pitch, the Founder would take over, the project would grind to a halt and we would be back to tallying up the number of phone calls we made each day to justify our existence.

The VP finally found someone who did cold-calling as a profession. The VP trained Cold-Call Gal on how to use our web-based products and gave her a list of prospects. Cold-Call Gal would then e-mail a summary report to us once a week noting which prospects were cold, warm or hot and, the hottest, which were the ones she had been able to schedule for a product demonstration. This was a big help and the type of support we needed, but the Founder cancelled Cold-Call Gal because the Board of Directors didn't want to pay what they thought was a high, hourly wage. Cold-Call Gal was generating leads that, with some work, we could convert to sales. The Founder wanted Cold-Call Gal to go on commission and Cold-Call Gal declined. Someone should have done the math.

About this time, the Founder and the Chairman convinced the Board that the Company should acquire a traditional consulting company to generate revenue until the web-based products took off. The Chairman wanted the Founder to spend time raising money from investors to acquire the consulting company. They both took the VP to the deli, which the First Salesman had nicknamed the Executive Suite, and they talked the VP into taking over the Sales function to free up the time of the Founder for the bigger picture. Suddenly, I had the Sequel to the Head of Sales from my old job.

Even though the VP, who could be a pill, was not really cut out for Sales, she somehow had figured out that it was a discipline not an art and she started putting structure into our days and into our approach to customers. She correctly claimed that the only sales technique that we had any success with was the beta test process. The VP wanted us to select specific targets, give them a free two-week trial of the web-products and then try to convert them to customers. Well, this was way too labor intensive for me because in order for the customer to get any value out of the products they had to be trained how to use them. I pushed the training off on the VP and the CSR by telling them they were better at it than we were, and the First Salesman and I only had to get involved in the introduction and then the close.

We got results because this was a low risk way for potential customers to get comfortable with an expensive, high-tech product. But when the Founder finished raising the funds for the acquisition of the consulting company, the Sales function was taken back from the VP and that was that.

Well, my ten-foot waves turned into two-foot waves. Eventually my life was such a misery that I quit the Company. I have sincerely doubted my ability to sell anything to anyone ever since. This has made my mother happy because she finally has had the opportunity to say, "See, I wanted you to become a doctor, but would you listen??"

Here are the lessons that I learned about Sales working for the Company:

- Firing the guy who has experience and contacts in your industry to "save" money will turn out to be more expensive than you can imagine.

- Selling a high-tech product to a low-tech industry takes time and hand holding. You have got to find ways to reduce the risk the customer perceives in the product. Sell the product to your industry big-mouths first who then tout how smart they themselves are for using your product. This is not rocket science.

- Asking people to sell a high-risk product without any support staff, marketing materials, price sheet or proven sales pitch is just insane.

- Do the math before dismissing anyone as valuable as Cold-Call Gal.

Chapter 12: Merger Fervor

Contributor: The Acquired Senior Vice President (ASVP)

Narrator: *The Acquired Senior Vice President (ASVP) merged his consulting practice with the Company at about year two and a half in the Company's lifecycle. He did not experience the energy, success, and enthusiasm of the earliest days of the Company. Rather, he and his employees witnessed only the downward spiral of the worst days of the Company as the pre-merger gleaming promises of the Founder and the Chairman turned out to be absolutely undeliverable. Here the ASVP describes the business lessons he learned from his painful association with the Company.*

Finally, *someone* had shown interest in buying my consulting practice!

My firm was the Company's first of two acquisitions and I, post-merger, was its Acquired Senior Vice President (ASVP) in charge of the Professional Services division (which I had initially called the Consulting arm of the Company). I was quickly made aware, by the Founder and by the Chairman, that the word "consulting" should never cross my lips again. It was a term the

105

venture capital community hated. It seems that a "consulting" practice, in the eyes of venture capitalists, is too labor intensive to ever be considered by them as a possible investment. Consulting, by their definition, cannot be profitable or "scalable". Nor can it then be taken public or sold to the highest bidder. No matter that my practice was profitable and my employees and I enjoyed very substantial annual bonuses. So, "Professional Services" it was.

Why did I want to sell my firm? There were a number of reasons, some personal and others professional. It had been a long haul for me. I had bought the consulting practice from my father eight years previously and had grown the company quite handsomely. Mind you, I had worked my staff and myself to the bone. But, we were a group of folks that had worked together for a number of years and we genuinely cared for one another. I shared the profits quite nicely with them, both through our annual bonuses as well as a profit-sharing plan. I knew that a team that stayed together should be rewarded for its tenure because it was a team that worked efficiently and profitably. I always liked to say that we worked together so well that much of our communication was done in shorthand. With little explanation, my employees knew what to expect from one another and me, and we worked together *brilliantly*.

But, I was tired, and hoped that selling my firm would be a way for me to share rather than shoulder most of the responsibility. And I wanted to work with others to grow a larger firm of which my consulting practice would be just a part of a more diverse business. Also, a merger with another related and growing company presented a new challenge for me. Though I was busy in my consultant role, truthfully, I was also a little bored.

It was becoming apparent to me that, without a serious infusion of cash, my consulting practice was too small to offer our customers cutting-edge technology. Further, we did not have a dedicated sales staff, and I was reluctant to develop one because of the extended training time it typically took to get a new person trained to sell our services. I began to think that my acquirer should be a technology-based firm because heck, the dot.com rage was the *happening* place to be. I assumed that there were technology-based companies who were trying to acquire a related consulting practice to add credibility, steady revenue, and a wider customer base to their business and I began to look for them.

I was initially contacted by another firm about a potential merger, but I had reservations because the "fit" seemed wrong. As I proceeded with my due-diligence process, which I defined as a long, careful, close look at the sales pipeline, customer references, and financial health of the acquiring company, I came to understand that the President of the firm which had contacted me was in his mid-60s and wanted to retire. He wanted me to run *his firm,* which was losing money. So much for sharing the responsibility! Needless to say, I was disappointed and I pulled out of the potential deal.

I was next courted by the Founder of the Company, who offered me a 100% stock deal, a risk I, being quite conservative, was not willing to take. The Founder wanted, in essence, to acquire my $2 million firm by giving me stock in the start-up Company. The Company stock at the time had a value, the Founder said, of $1.80 per share. This "value" was assigned to the stock by a vote of the Board of Directors – all of whom were investors in the Company. I turned the offer down when the Founder stated that the Company did not have any cash to offer. But the Founder, continued, in a most entrepreneurial fashion, to rationalize why I should be interested in a 100% stock deal, the arguments of which were clearly illogical but impressively manipulative. I pointed out that there was no market for the Company stock and, therefore, it was not possible for me to sell it and turn it into cash. The Founder continued to circle back around to me with forceful, ridiculous counter-arguments. I continued to say no.

Months went by before I heard from the Founder again but this time I was asked what terms I *would* be willing to consider. I put together an offer that I would accept if the deal could be made. It was a mix of cash and stock, which made me more comfortable. Also, the Company had access, or so I was told, to a larger pot of gold. The Founder wanted to acquire more related companies and spur greater revenue growth for the combined Companies. How could I lose being the first to be acquired? Nothing like getting in on the ground floor!

We proceeded with acquisition discussions because I thought the Founder and the start-up Company had lots of access to venture capital. The Founder had raised and spent an initial $6.0 million to develop a web-based screening tool that would help streamline our industry's critical decision-making process. With the web-based product now partially developed, the Founder thought it prudent to purchase a Professional Services (but really, it's a Consulting) firm to be able to more fully serve the clients of the Company. We would now offer both web-based products AND consulting services to our industry.

Another reason I believed there was access to capital was that the Founder and the Chairman appeared to be quite wealthy, and I was naively impressed. The Founder owned two homes in an outrageously expensive gated community and drove a huge, black BMW – the gigantic 700 series model. The Chairman had made millions founding and growing a health care company (no relation or applicability to our industry) that he eventually sold to the public market. He drove a Mercedes (blue) and his personal second car was a new Jaguar. His second home was in a luxurious mountain resort. So, how could I and my wonderful loyal employees lose? Losing was easy:

- Things were NOT as they appeared or as they were presented, and

- I was less than objective, being clouded by what I perceived as the Founder and the Chairman's history of success. I confused personal wealth with corporate wealth which was a huge mistake.

But, finally, my consulting firm and I were acquired by the Founder and the Chairman for cash and stock.

Once the acquisition had been finalized I realized, unfortunately later rather than sooner, that there were fatal flaws in the acquiring Company. Though the Company appeared to have a large, talented staff roster and customers who were some of the greatest in our industry, there were serious problems simmering below the surface. Many of these flaws I should have realized during my due-diligence period with the Company; others were only revealed to me as the businesses merged, and some were just plain misrepresentations by the Founder and the Chairman. These flaws boil down to the following critical seven issues:

1. The Founder and the Chairman believed that raising money was more important than generating sales revenue: Was I wrong to think that a successful business needed sales revenue? Why was the sales group treated as a "wicked stepsister" in the Company and why was it always second to raising money from investors? Why, in fact, did sales seem like a pariah? Didn't the Company need sales and rapidly growing sales?

2. The Company sales team knew little about our business and our industry. Another disconcerting revelation was that the existing, three-person sales team had no work experience in our industry, especially the consulting side. They had few industry contacts and no hands-on industry experience, which stunned me. Their lack of knowledge kept them from making significant sales contributions to the web-based component of our merged Company, though not from a lack of trying. The Founder wanted to save money, and so hired three inexpensive people rather than one expensive industry professional. Those poor three guys were hounded eight hours a day until they managed to close some low-price subscriptions for our web-based products. But closing those deals was ugly.

3. The Company Employees were Second-Class Citizens. I always ran a business in which I respected my employees. If a job had to get done, I didn't care what your title was, we ALL had to pitch in. In this new Company, management was not supposed to help with what were perceived by the Founder and Chairman as menial tasks. Rather, senior management was to pontificate on direction for the Company, not that most of the senior management knew enough about our business to pontificate on direction. They merely spouted their own theories. But what was even scarier was that the Founder and Chairman had NO concept of what motivated employees. It was their feeling that employees should WANT to work for the company, which is fair enough, but that the Company owed NOTHING to the employees. Sometimes not even a pay check.

I had never debated with myself that my way of relating to my employees was correct; I *knew* it was. I had proven it through the profits we had made and shared year, after year, after year! And I noticed when I arrived at the Company that many of the staff were extremely self-motivated, so much so that they enabled and covered up the lack of senior management skills.

4. There was a big double standard in what was expected of our clients and what we owed our vendors. Why was it all right to not pay our bills to vendors for months at a time, but to expect that our clients should pay us in fifteen days? In fact, the Founder would become indignant if our clients did not pay us immediately. I was required to call my long-term clients and beg for money, a practice which disgusted me and one which my clients never had encountered with me or my firm, pre-acquisition.

5. The Company took tried-and-true processes and destroyed them. The Company had been in business for only two years when they acquired my practice and me, while my firm had been in business for 36 years. However, all of our processes were discarded for ones that were not tested and:

- Did not make sense in our business;
- Were processes that many of us were convinced would not work and, most importantly;
- Were a roadblock for getting work done and invoiced.

I have termed this time in the Company's history as "going from process to chaos!"

Even today it is difficult for me to ascertain whether the Company's top-level managers were misunderstood managerial geniuses but just didn't get it, or, were more likely just inserting themselves into something they knew nothing about.

6. The Company had an arrogant senior management team. Simply put, why did management have greater expectations of their employees than they did of themselves? As an entrepreneur, I always felt that it was my responsibility to lead by example. Why didn't they? Why was it that this senior management team NEVER admitted to its mistakes? I came to believe that the level of managerial arrogance was so high, and the level of experience so low, that the Company was doomed.

7. The Company was running on financial fumes. The balance of the Company's struggle boiled down to this. There was never ANY money to hire new staff, fulfill the incoming projects, upgrade employees' computers, offer additional training to employees, provide raises, or to pay incentive bonuses.... ANYTHING! Why wasn't there any money? And more importantly, why didn't the Board of Directors care how the Company spent the little cash it had? What kind of corporate excesses were happening? A very small example of poor planning and ridiculous excess was the overnight mail expense for sending the Board members their Board packages instead of e-mailing them the meeting materials a few days before the meeting. A second, telling, but rather embarrassing example of excess is the marketing splash that the merger of our two firms made at the annual industry convention. There was advertising, promotion, promotional products, interviews, and dinner and cocktails which had originally been planned to cost $30,000 but ended up costing $60,000. Was there ever a budget drawn up or a cost/benefit calculation done? And this occurred at a time when funds for payroll were in crisis.

Oh my God, what had I gotten my beloved employees and myself into? Our collective professional reputations were in jeopardy. What had once been a fast paced but financially rewarding place to work was no longer fun, but contentious. I can recall the Company's Vice President of Operations screaming obscenities about "processes" to my Accounting Manager (a well-respected, 26-year employee). And keep in mind, the VP of Operations knew NOTHING about accounting. He ran a sandwich shop prior to his position at the Company and it was his wife who kept the books.

After two years, the consulting (I can now use the word again) arm of the business began to disintegrate. First, I lost my "Cash Cow" who was sick of his treatment and the lack of respect from COO3, who could not have cared less about his contribution to the firm. Next, went my Saintly Operations Manager of the Chicago office who needed more stability and a guaranteed paycheck ("Why is that so important to her?" asked the Founder who owned two homes and drove a (black) BMW.) The final nail in my coffin was the departure of the Vice President in charge of the Chicago office. When I warned the Founder and the Chairman that this talented young man was looking for other employment, they arrogantly told me that he would never find a job that paid as well as the one at the Company in what was now a slowing economy. Not only did he land a more prestigious job, but he is now being paid 25% more than when he was with the Company! So, what did I learn? Plenty!

- No Sales = No Business. Seems self-evident but you would be amazed at the number of people who don't get this.

- Acquisition due-diligence is not simply about understanding the financial viability of the acquirer or the acquired. Another part of the due-diligence equation is the managerial integrity and expertise of the merging firms. Do you have shared values when it comes to how you are going to treat your employees? I was horrified to discover that the Founder, the Chairman and I did not.

- A company that does not value its employees is a company that is doomed to fail. Let your employees do what they do best. I learned a personal lesson, which is that I can *never* work again for a company that has such little respect for its employees.

- All employees, including senior management, should have measurable goals and objectives, and there should be consequences for not achieving these goals. Yes, I know this, too, is obvious but the Company did not know, understand, or believe this.

Chapter 13: The Robot in the Grey Flannel Suit

Contributor: The Marketing/Public Relations Consultant

> *Narrator:* *The Marketing Maven was a seasoned professional who knew everyone in the industry. She understood the challenge of getting a small, new company noticed at a national convention with 35,000 attendees. Her industry contacts were used to make sure the Company was seen as prescient, and she called in a lot of personal vouchers to give the Company great exposure in the industry press. Well, as they say, "No good deed goes unpunished."*

My relationship with the Company started out incestuously. Here is my story. I had been the Director of Marketing and Public Relations (PR) for a prestigious firm in the Company's industry for about four years. An Independent Contractor, who would eventually become the Founder of the Company, was hired to work on a specific project for us. In the first week on the job, the Independent Contractor walked over to my office. I was up to my eyeballs meeting a press release deadline but the Independent

Contractor was hungry. Surely, I could run out and bring a sandwich back for the Independent Contractor. I found the request inappropriate and I declined. I was busy, for God's sake, and I reported to the President – not to the Independent Contractor.

Over the next couple of weeks, the Independent Contractor tried the "get me a sandwich" request on just about everyone in the office, with the exception of the President, with no idea how to relate to people in the office. None. The Independent Contractor had no concept of building working relationships. Zero. And felt entitled to use our co-workers as servants. Totally. Then the Independent Contractor teamed up with the only other obnoxious person in the office to work on the special project. I was the first one they approached with demands for help. Seriously.

I went to the President and said that I would become annoyingly violent if I had to work with them. It was them-or-me time. He told them that I was too swamped to help them, and that they were to use the services of our remote office for whatever they needed to get the job done. He wisely also approved hiring an assistant for them so the rest of us could get our work done. Not a great beginning with the future Founder, so you may be wondering how I ended up working for the Company. Here comes the incestuous part.

After eighteen months or so, the Independent Contractor left us to form the Company, and a year later, my boss sold our firm to a large company and he "retired." I resigned and opened my own Marketing/PR practice. The Founder then called my old boss and asked him to become the Executive Vice President (EVP) of Sales and Marketing of the Company. Retirement bored him so he said, "Yes." I later heard that the first convention was good, and that it generated a lot of solid interest in the Company.

I was surprised, then, when eight months later, the Founder and my former boss called me. They had run a series of ads that were costly and produced nothing in the way of revenue, web site traffic or interest in the Company. Would I meet with them, review the advertising that had been done, and offer suggestions? In a private phone call, I checked things out and discovered that the EVP was a buffer between the Founder and the staff, so things would not be too bad working with the Founder. The EVP said he needed my professional help. I said sure, thinking why not?

I met with them, looked at the ads they had had produced, and critiqued them. The Company had just done a Treasure Hunt on their web site for a Grand Prize lottery, and it had generated no interest. None. Well, I told them that video games like the web Treasure Hunt appeal to a small subset of people and not to anyone in our industry which is full of Type A, hyper people who think they are all too busy and too important to be caught playing a web-game. In addition, and before this meeting, I had tried to find the hidden Treasure myself and failed beyond belief. I was not surprised that they got no response, but the Founder was angry and, I think embarrassed at this failure. After this meeting, the

Founder asked me to submit a proposal outlining what I could do for the Company with a fee schedule.

I sent the Company a creative proposal because I understood the potential of the products they were developing, and I still enjoyed working with the EVP. My proposal was accepted and there I, incestuously, was – working a couple-days-per-week as a consultant to the Company, the Founder, and my old boss, now the EVP, on what I thought was going to be an exciting project.

It was not easy dealing with the Founder this time either. I should mention that my initial proposal sat on the receptionist's desk for ten days because the Founder was too busy to read it. Then the EVP called me to ask why I hadn't returned the Founder's telephone call? What call? So, I phoned the Founder right away to apologize. Profusely. And I was accused of being non-responsive. We got past that, but barely. Then the Founder told the EVP that my proposal was full of typos. This time I made an appointment and went to the Company office to talk with the Founder. What typos? I don't make typos. Yes, they hired me, but it was a rocky start.

The nature of my work for the Company was that I was to attend meetings with the Founder, the Chairman, and the EVP and then go off-site to be creative and come back with marketing alternatives for them to discuss and select/reject. At our first meeting, we looked at the ads the Company had run, so I could be brought up to date quickly. I picked up the Treasure Hunt contest postcard and asked the Founder and the Chairman what the goal of the contest was. They both looked at me like I was speaking in Farsi. Honestly.

This was a question I often asked new clients to get the drift of their thinking and marketing strategy. Was the goal of the contest to drive traffic to the web-site, make the office phones ring, develop name recognition, or achieve the marketer's top prize which is word-of-mouth advertising? Or was it a combination of those things? I really believe that Marketing/PR should produce results. It can, you know. It should produce what the senior executives want – more eyes on the web-site, more interest in the products/services, more sales, more customers, more something. The Founder and the Chairman looked at me as though just getting the postcards that announced the Treasure Hunt to the post office was an achievement in itself. I did not agree. The Chairman made an off-hand remark about not knowing what type of marketing was going to work with a new Company and a new product. I think the quote was that they had been, "throwing things against the wall to see what would stick." Hello? I could not have disagreed more.

If the goal of the Treasure Hunt was to drive traffic to the web-site, what did they want people to do/see/experience/learn when they were on the web-site? If the intent of the contest was to make the phones ring with questions about the web products, who was going to answer the phones and what script were they to use to pitch the services of the Company? If the goal was name recognition, there were far better ways to get that than their postcard Treasure Hunt. I believe that all elements must support achieving the marketing goal, and the plan must be comprehensive. What was the goal of the postcard and did they think they had achieved it? This is a straight forward, common sense question. Really. The Founder and the Chairman stared at me.

Okay. When the senior executives are vague about what they want Marketing/PR to do for them, I talk with the people in the trenches. I met with the sales guys, the customer service rep, and the VP – all people who actually talk with the customers. A pattern began to emerge for me. The web product was an innovative, expensive product, and the thoughtful PR pieces that had been done to explain this new product had gotten the most customer response. PR was what got the phones ringing and the potential customers interested in testing this New Thing.

Now, let me tell you how this works. My job is to call all the trade journal editors that I know, and I know them all, and spin a couple of story lines to whet their appetites about doing an article featuring the Company. The editors may then agree to do an article and to interview the Founder and quote the Founder extensively – there is your PR. The Company then reciprocates by purchasing advertising space in the trade journal on a schedule that makes sense for the Company and its advertising budget. I, then, develop ads that reinforce the PR message – maybe the ads even look like PR pieces. But the point I am making here is one of reciprocity. The Company works with the editors and they work with the Company because the Company might buy advertising space. There is no way the Chairman and the Founder ever understood this. They insisted that PR is "free." No way.

I had a Founder and a Chairman who resisted and resented buying advertising space in the trade magazines that were featuring the Company in articles right alongside the long-time established industry players. While it was critical to the Founder to be photographed and quoted in the trade magazines, it apparently was of no importance to support the trade journals that were in turn supporting the Company's early days. Explain that to an editor.

The disconnect between the world of Marketing/PR and the world that the Founder inhabited went beyond advertising. The Founder, I discovered, felt that deadlines were for employees, not Founders and Chairmen. My business is totally deadline driven. PR has deadlines, advertising has deadlines, and conventions which are held on specific days have deadlines. Time after time, I had to call an editor, an advertising department, or convention staff and beg for an extra day because the Founder was late. Oh, yes, I routinely built two to three extra days into any schedule that involved the Founder. But those were my deadlines, not those of the Founder who did not operate in a world of deadlines. I blew right through all the favors anyone in the industry owed me in a matter of six months. The Founder ignored the fact that my professional relationships "enabled" the Company's extremely unprofessional behavior. When I had used up all my industry chits, the Founder then suggested that I simply lie. Lie? No way, not in this small industry.

I know what you are thinking – why didn't I walk? The Company owed me too much money – how oh-my-God is that?

The final straw was the merger with a professional services firm. Not the merger itself – that actually appeared smart. I loved the contrast of the merger. Hi-tech whiz kid marries old, established, traditional consulting firm. The whole attraction-of-opposites spin. Getting my mind around the message was fun. It was the promotional plan for the merger that was the last straw for me. The general idea was that we were to announce the merger at the second annual, national convention the Company would attend. I achieved a flurry of PR in the three months preceding the convention but I was having a hard time getting the Founder and the Chairman to focus on the merger message for the advertising.

There were several intriguing angles. The new company represented as a high-tech robot but dressed in a "consultant's" traditional grey flannel suit, fedora, and shades. Well, you get the picture. Week after week I brought the Founder and the Chairman different ideas for the deadline-looming advertising. They both ignored me. Then, when the deadline got very close, they instructed me to dumb everything down. No buffed metallic robot – no soft grey flannel suit – too complex – our industry will never get it – keep it simple. Then the Founder had a "vision" that the Chairman agreed with. The vision for the lead ad was that of two men shaking hands on a putting green. That will convey the message of the merger? Absolutely. Not.

I sympathize with your gasp. Two guys on a golf course? Good old scions of the country club? Neither merging company had any relation to golf! A photo of the hairy legs of two guys in golf shoes? Who will pause and look at that visual? The whole idea was stupid and confusing.

The convention's deadline was so close now, I barely had time to execute let alone argue with the two of them. I had been neatly stalled and maneuvered into an awful compromise. The Founder was the whole advertising department – the designer, copy writer, and entire creative team. So, the putting green it was, and everyone at the convention knew that I was the Marketing/PR person for the Company. Several "friends"/peers/competitors suggested that my creative spiral was in a downward direction. It took all of my will power but I kept my mouth shut.

Here are my who-would-believe-I-got-myself-into-this-mess lessons:

- Marketing/PR can produce results if you set clear goals. What do you want? The Company phones to ring? Increased hits to your web-site? Industry word-of-mouth? State your goals and then use marketing and PR to achieve those goals.

- There must be what I call a continuous loop – company goals loop to marketing tactics which loop to the marketing message which loops to employees who interact with the customers who loop to the Company sometimes because of Marketing/PR. Everything needs to be on-message, all the time. But for this to work, the top executives must make clear decisions about the marketing goals of the Company. They cannot resent the marketing person who picks up the postcard announcing the Treasure Hunt and asks, "What was your goal when you sent out this direct mail piece?"

- In a deadline driven business, remove if possible the people who consider themselves above meeting deadlines, regardless of their titles.

- Don't ever risk your professional reputation by subjecting yourself to the unreasonable demands of absurd individuals. Ever.

Chapter 14: Who is The Fairest of Them All? The Narcissistic Paradox

Contributors: ASVP and CTO2

Narrator: *Narcissism is hopeless because it appears incurable. They are masterful manipulators. They believe they are special and should only have to associate with other special people. Narcissists cannot be admired enough by others and cannot deal with as much as the faintest criticism. They need to keep people off-balance so one day you are essential to their well-being and the next day they really cannot remember your name.*

The narcissist views the world as a win or lose situation. If someone else wins then, by definition, the narcissist loses. An employee, then, can never win because the narcissist boss becomes diminished when that happens. Everything is about them and the employee will give, give, give until that employee is empty.

Here ASVP and CTO2, both of whom have dealt with narcissistic family members, tell us what the siren song of these narcissistic personalities is and how to partially protect your Company if it is infected.

Narrator: Let's start with your qualifications for discussing narcissistic behavior. What life experiences have you had that lead you to believe the Founder might be so afflicted?

ASVP: Well, simply my background is that I have a very narcissistic father and I know that my personality and my likelihood of getting hoodwinked, if you will, are very much based on that. It has been a life-defining issue for me.

CTO2: In my case, it was my mother and my stepfather who were "so afflicted."

Narrator: Has a therapist ever told you that your parent was narcissistic?

*ASVP***:** Oh, my therapists have all said that my father is extremely narcissistic and, indeed, has a borderline personality disorder which can have some similarities with narcissism. For example, a borderline personality tends to split people into categories. You are either good or you are bad, you are nothing in between. And in the Company, you were either with the Founder or you were not, there was no in between. Any criticism, no matter how minor, signaled to the Founder that you were not loyal.

*CTO2***:** I have had several different therapists off and on over a 20 to 30-year period. In all cases when I have described sets of family circumstances and behavior, these professionals have defined my mother and my stepfather as being narcissistic. My brother, who is a year older than I, went back to school and got his Masters degree in psychology. He did his thesis on our mother and based on his clinical background was able to categorize her as narcissistic. I also have done a lot of reading on my own about psychology at large and specifically have read and studied narcissism. All the books comport that I am the adult child of a narcissist.

Narrator: When did you suspect that the Founder might be thusly afflicted?

ASVP: It took me almost a year to figure that out which is very classic behavior for the child of a narcissist. I knew something was wrong because my reality did not match the Founder's reality but I didn't know why. I should have known and I should have known it immediately.

CTO2: I feel that a lot of entrepreneurs are almost predisposed to being narcissistic. To be entrepreneurial means that you want to project your world view on the world rather than accept somebody else's world view. My interactions with the Founder, when we shared office space back when the Company was just an idea, showed me personality tendencies that were clearly in the narcissistic realm. So, I knew going into the Company as a consultant, that the Founder was afflicted. I saw it clearly but I didn't realize how much pull that narcissistic behavior still had on me. In my case, I went in with my eyes open but I was unable to do anything to deny the pull. It was during this time with the Founder that I gained some additional insight into how I was still operating in that mode and then I proceeded to break out of it.

ASVP: You know what is interesting? I am like a bee to honey when it comes to narcissistic personalities. I am attracted to them. It is like a magnetic pull.

CTO2: Yes, that had been the case with me but I no longer feel that I am attracted to this kind of behavior.

Narrator: How did you break the pull?

CTO2: Mostly through reflecting. And through pain. The pain of experiencing it and thinking, "Wait a minute, I don't need this anymore." And I finally understand how important my own needs, wants and concerns are as opposed to always subjugating them to someone else's.

Narrator: But, ASVP, you are still like a bee to honey? Is that because it takes you a while to identify the disorder?

ASVP: Yes, I would say so but if I think about it I would notice that if there is an attraction, I had better ask myself what that attraction is. It might be that I am responding to somebody that has these huge needs and I will subjugate mine to theirs out of force of habit.

Narrator: What was your internal response to your hunch that the Founder was so afflicted? What did you find attractive about this disorder that drew you in?

ASVP: The Founder's enthusiasm allowed me to not see beyond it because I was attracted to that enthusiasm. However, the enthusiasm was indicative of something else which was "what can you do for me?"

CTO2:   I think there is a charisma about most entrepreneurs, and I think there is a set of people who choose entrepreneurial or start-up situations. It is largely a different breed of people who seem to go into start-ups from those who stay in main stream businesses. The draw for me was that it's a more exciting life even though it's a more painful life; it is a more exciting interaction even though it is measurably more painful because you are an indispensable co-worker one day and an ignored serf the next. In my case, although earlier I described it as a pull or a draw, I also thought it was a realistic opportunity to be involved in a viable Internet company. There was good money involved but I set aside what I knew would be a fatal flaw, a red flag, and said "Oh, well, let's go ahead" because of the other good things such as the business concept itself, the salary, and the stock options.

ASVP: See, that's the difference. You had that awareness going in and I did not. I should have, but I didn't.

CTO2:   It's easier in hindsight to say that I knew but probably the decision was mushier. With hindsight I can see that I ignored a big, red flag. At the time I was asked to join the Company as a consultant, I did write the Founder a letter explaining why I wasn't going to accept the offer. In that letter, I was critical of the Founder's executive capabilities and style. I said, "You don't delegate, you just have a bunch of personal assistants running around you," but then I flew in the face of my own observations and became a consultant to the Company.

Narrator: What was common to you both, then, was that the enthusiasm and the excitement the Founder generated were key. Another commonality you both had was that the Company looked like a viable business opportunity and, therefore, you were intrigued.

CTO2: Yes, actually. I didn't really believe that the Founder would totally act out narcissistically. One of the characteristics of narcissists is that they make you feel that you are integral and important to them. When they focus their attention on you they make you feel indispensable and they talk about how much they need you. Then, without warning or justification you become invisible to them. Your solutions and the fact that you stepped in to save them are simply ignored. You are just thrown out to be replaced by the person they need next.

ASVP: That's right – here again, it is either black or white with them – there is no gray.

CTO2: There was a fellow I consulted for who was quite a successful executive and grew his company into several billion dollars. He was a mentor of mine. When I used to interact with him, I taught him "computing." He would always say, "Oh, you are such a genius." Then one time we went out to lunch and we happened to be in a restaurant of which he was co-owner and he said to the chef, "Oh, you are such a genius." Then I noticed a few other times when I was with him and other people that he would often say, "Oh, you are such a genius." What I came to realize was that he used some stock words to make you feel really good. So finally, I stopped taking being a genius personally.

ASVP: You know, I had an interaction with the Founder not too long after I left and in which the Founder said, "Boy, have you lost a lot of weight." And I said, "Thank you!" When I went home and said to my partner, "The Founder noticed that I lost a lot of weight," my partner said, "What does the Founder want from you?" But I was still thinking, "Wow, what a compliment!" I just can't seem to get past it. It was very obvious to my partner that the Founder had complimented me to make me feel good and to make it easier to manipulate me into doing something for the Company but it was not obvious to me and it should have been.

Narrator: What do you find repulsive about this disorder?

ASVP: What I find repulsive is that it keeps everyone in chaos and destroys self-esteem.

CTO2: I agree. It creates a lot of pain and havoc. The unconscious creates a lot of harm and it creates a lot of harm around everybody. I think it is ultimately destructive or self-destructive and therefore if the Founder self-destructs then the organization is self-destructing. I think it is an interesting paradox because a lot of entrepreneurs exhibit narcissism and there is a real set up for failure here which is probably why the "Founder's Trap" is such a diagnosed organizational problem. Founder's Trap, if you recall from Adizes *Corporate Lifecycles*, is when the Founder completely dominates the organization and is the company's biggest asset and biggest liability simultaneously. We had a classic symptom of Founder's Trap in the Company in that we had a Board selected and then controlled by the Founder. What happened? They saw no compelling reason to insert a COO and direct that person's skills inside the Company and re-direct the Founder's energy outside the Company. The Board was controlled and manipulated by the Founder. This is a classic symptom of Founder's Trap. I am currently interacting with an entrepreneur who is not at all narcissistic and, interestingly, he is not the founding entrepreneur; rather he is the professional manager who is coming in as the CEO. This is a big difference. The fellow has already transitioned the company to the next stage of the business lifecycle.

ASVP: Let me ask a question that I do not know the answer to. Is the Founder's ability to remain with the Company as an executive due to the Founder's narcissism?

CTO2: Yes, I think so, because they are expert manipulators. And one of the keys to successfully staying put is to manipulate the heck out of everyone around you, above you and below you.

Narrator: Once you realized what was going on, did you try to distance yourself from the Founder?

CTO2: Oh, yeah!

ASVP: Oh, yeah!

Narrator: And how did that work?

***CTO2*:** Well, in my case, because I was a consultant and not expected to be in the office full-time, I learned evasive behaviors. In that wide-open workspace I would avoid walking by the Founder's desk or office. When heading out to a meeting I quickly learned that the Founder would grab whoever was there and engage them like a life raft, so I stayed far away. I am pretty good at saying no and I did say no.

***ASVP*:** It took me a while to set boundaries with the Founder. In the beginning, I would stay at the office until 11:00pm at which time the Founder would insist on opening a bottle of wine. I had to put boundaries on that fast. And once I did, things were a little bit better. I blush to recall that I would slink out of the office at the end of the day so the Founder wouldn't see me and grab me on the way out.

***CTO2*:** Anybody joining a start-up business should be aware they could end up working for a narcissist Founder. Setting boundaries is an appropriate, necessary, protective strategy.

Narrator: What are your personal keys to the narcissistic personality and what will be your professional response the next time you encounter this?

***CTO2*:** I think, next time, I will just go in judiciously. I can't say I am going to completely avoid narcissists because they are involved in so many start-ups. And I can't say that I will avoid start-ups because they are all I have ever done.

ASVP: I am going to try to diagnose that person earlier and react to my judgment earlier.

CTO2: We have identified an interesting paradox here. I will paraphrase George Bernard Shaw, "Reasonable people adapt to their circumstances; unreasonable people try to change their circumstances. Therefore, all progress stems from unreasonable people." But there is some element of that in our experience with the Founder and it's a paradox. In a way, the unreasonableness was a strength – vis-à-vis the vision for the business. Almost any character trait we have is a strength and a weakness – a double-edged sword. It was a great strength externally but a serious weakness internally.

ASVP: It also makes it impossible to become friendly with the narcissist because they are one-upping you constantly, regardless of the experience or issue that you want to share with them. The Founder has endless wealth but the Founder's cash financial situation was always worse than mine and I was the employee. I would say to the Founder, "I need to be paid," and the response would be, "Well, I haven't been paid in a very long time, my finances are in really bad shape, my credit rating stinks and my credit card has been shut off, blah, blah, blah." There was no discussion and you would have to come back to your issue and say, "Yes, I understand your problem, but I really do need to be paid." That takes an employee a tremendous amount of energy, constant watchfulness, and unrelenting, fruitless looping back to your topic. It is exhausting.

CTO2: I keep thinking back about how I rationalized my decision to join the Company. Things were fairly complicated because on the surface the Chairman looked credible, and the Board looked credible, and they seemed to be endorsing the Founder. I didn't do any reference checks and did not realize that those people were all just referencing each other. I looked at the Chairman from the outside and saw that he was running his own rather successful company and I knew a little bit about his resume. But I didn't go the full step of conducting due diligence on him before I accepted him as a reference for the Founder.

ASVP: That's why I am not sure I would not be blinded again. We had three pretty big hitters from our industry in one room – the Board room – and it ultimately was no guarantee that they would make the right decisions for the Company.

CTO2: If there is one theme that has gotten me into more trouble in my life than anything else it's when I have been referred to somebody by someone I really know and trust. I project the trust I have with the second person onto the new person. That has gotten me into trouble so many times. If I am going to put my heart and soul and energy into something I have got to do better due diligence. We are so used to thinking that the employer checks on us but I think it is really important for any follower to research the leader.

Narrator: Is there any cure for the narcissist?

ASVP: Absolutely not. Narcissists typically suffer very low self-esteem and need to be right at all times to bolster their ego. In the narcissist's mind there is only one way, their way, so don't wait for them to heal themselves because they don't think they are ill.

CTO2: Well, I don't think there is a cure for the individual but I do think that there is a cure for the organization. Having a strong COO is important and having the Founder/Entrepreneur have an outward focus rather than be inwardly in command of the company is critical. The lifecycle of the company should move from a dictatorship to a constitutional monarchy to get out of the Founder's Trap. Now this Founder didn't permit that to happen but, honestly, none of us were insisting on it because I think we were all assuming that the Board would eventually do what was obvious to us – either replace the Founder or insert a professional COO or CEO. The next time I get involved in this type of situation of leadership dysfunction I am going to need to see a strong COO with defined tasks and a clear role. There needs to be a contractual, corporate, organizational boundary, not just employees with personal boundaries to prevent the craziness from seeping in.

Narrator: Here is the last question: Do you think narcissists are aware of their affliction?

ASVP: Absolutely not – they have no concept.

CTO2: I agree. The narcissistic personality is not going to self-correct. And the purpose of this book is to help others learn what to look for and understand the corporate structure that should be in place in certain circumstances like these.

ASVP: Yet the entrepreneur/narcissist may have qualities that are very important for the organization.

CTO2: They do and here again is our paradox. Many Founders are unsuitable as managers – it is the rare ones who are good managers.

Here are some lessons from this conversation, then:

- It is unlikely that you can escape the narcissist. Sooner or later you will have a family member, acquaintance, or co-worker who has this peculiar disorder. Learn the symptoms and if you come away from every conversation with a particular co-worker and you feel confused, baffled, and off-center, consider that you may have just found a narcissist.

- Protect yourself by putting physical and emotional distance between you and the narcissist. Develop and practice the skill of avoidance with this person. Set firm boundaries between the two of you and keep them.

- If this person is your boss, look for another job. The narcissistic ailment is incurable and you will be drained, ignored, and left wondering if you are the one who is unstable. Your self-esteem will be in shreds. Do not put yourself through this. You cannot and will not win.

- Take responsibility for evaluating the people and company you are considering joining. Few work situations are perfect but they should all be tolerable. And if you ever have a job interview that begins with the interviewer saying, "Let me tell you about me and what I am doing," run for the hills.

Chapter 15: From Process to Chaos

Contributor: The Accountant of the Acquired Consulting Practice

---

Narrator: The Accountant who worked for the acquired consulting firm had twenty-five years of experience, all of it with that one consulting practice. She was efficient, organized, and had many systems in place at the time of the merger to process the often messy Accounts Receivable typical in a consulting practice. She had systems for tracking the cash flow of retainers, partial payments, final payments, and payments for work in addition to that of the original contract. The Accountant had an internal system for billing the consultant's time against jobs to determine project-by-project profitability. Her track record with Accounts Payable and vendors was impeccable, until the merger with the Company.

"What have we gotten ourselves into? The Founder and the Chairman of the Company that acquired us last week just spent two hours in our office and met with all of us in our conference room. Both of them assured us that this merger was going to be "nothing but positive" for all of us, so why do I feel as though I've just left a national sales convention? You know the kind… people in suits chanting the company mantra and believing in only themselves. Their smiles can sell you the world."

Perhaps it was the way the Founder and the Chairman dressed, or the fact that they flew into town just to have lunch with us and caught the next plane back home again. In that two-hour meeting they told us everything about themselves and answered a few general questions about our future together. They left us with more questions than answers, but I had the idea that they felt the meeting was successful. I have been teased for years for being the cheerleader in the office, but I have the feeling I just permanently misplaced my pompoms.

That first paragraph is a flashback of sorts, and I admit that, as the company cheerleader, I was embarrassed to have such serious doubts about the wisdom of the merger so early in the process. Where was my team spirit when I needed it most?

I was told about our merger with the high-tech start-up Company early, during the initial negotiation stage, because the documents that the prospective acquirers wanted to review were in my possession. Thanks to the excellent record-keeping requirements of the outside accounting firm that we had used for years, producing the volumes of documentation requested by the acquirers was easy, yet time consuming. "Volumes" of paperwork is not an exaggeration on my part. Over the course of two weeks, I copied nearly half the contents of our files for the acquirers and in triplicate, because the three principals each wanted their own copy. I spent several days at FedEx Office when our copier decided enough was enough. I was so swamped I had no time to react to the very real possibility that the small consulting company where I had worked for twenty-five years might be acquired.

My first encounter with the prospective buyers was during their initial visit to our office to review our financial statements. The Founder and CFO2 arrived accompanied by an independent auditor. I was confident that everything was in order and ready for their inspection. The auditor examined our records and then demanded more information.

He asked: "Where are your accrual schedules?"

I replied: "We have none as we are on a cash basis and use accruals only at year-end."

He asked: "Where are your amortization tables?"

I replied: "I do not do those because our outside accounting firm prepares them. Would you like me to get you a copy of them?"

He barked: "Three copies."

My answers appeared to be unsatisfactory because he then conferred with the Founder and CFO2. On the spot, I was told to create accrual schedules for Accounts Payable, Accounts Receivable and Payroll. I was told to have the amortization tables faxed over. And then copied, of course, three times.

It boggled my mind that our small consulting company could survive and be profitable without the monthly ritual of accrual and amortization tables yet the Founder and CFO2 could not make an acquisition decision without those reports. If they regularly generated detailed reports such as these themselves, how was it that they themselves were unprofitable?

In the weeks after our merger with the Company, I took the initiative to get consistency between my books and those of the Company. I e-mailed a list of questions regarding procedures and general ledger accounts. I asked what information they would need from me and on what schedule. After putting me off for a week, there was a conference call between CFO2, the Part Time Bookkeeper (PTB), and my old boss ASVP, and me. During this call, I learned that they had no general ledger and no chart of accounts. The software that the PTB was using was not designed for double entry bookkeeping; instead, they classified their expenditures into one of five categories. I asked a few questions and it became apparent that they had no feel for how the money in each classification was broken down or whether the amounts were above or below budget. It also became clear to me that while the Company had four office locations across the country, neither the Founder, CFO2 or the PTB could state the revenues and expenses of each office. And I became uneasy when CFO2 told me that a company as small as our combined Company did not need the level of detail that I had established.

I recall an overwhelming feeling of being almost invisible on that phone call and certainly extraneous to both the Founder and the PTB. They told me the PTB would be in touch with me over the next few weeks to re-divide our tasks, and that she would have a lot of questions for me. Okay – I expect transition in any merger, but didn't they, the Founder and CFO2, want to get to know me a bit to feel confident that I was trustworthy? I was going to be handling their Company's money, after all. There were clearly no accounting systems in place at the Company so why didn't they want to know about the ones we had used successfully for the past, oh say, twenty-five years? Not all the details, of course, but a high-level overview of Accounts Payable, Accounts Receivable, project tracking, and our 401-k plan.

Within the first five months of our merger, CFO2 was fired and replaced with a part-time controller. CFO2 had seemed content to let me do most of the work and endlessly asked me for calculations and projections that later had to be re-sent to him because he always misplaced them. I suspected, from his questions, or rather from his inability to clearly form his questions, that I knew more about bookkeeping than he did, despite his advanced degrees. My suspicions were confirmed when I made the trip to the West Coast so I could get to know the PTB better. I arrived in the office on the Tuesday after CFO2 had been fired and was given the task of sorting, categorizing, organizing, and filing all of the papers and reports that he had neglected. I found misplaced reports, duplicate reports, and an accounting task cheat sheet no one with a CPA should have needed.

In the first two years of our merger with the Company I worked sequentially with the PTB, CFO2, CFO3, an interim controller, two part-time controllers, and COO3 as well as an additional, occasional part-time bookkeeper. Please keep in mind as you read this that the merged Company was small with revenues of less than $3 million and about twenty-five employees.

With each change in the accounting/financial staff came a new approach to fixing what was wrong. Each person dissected the Company, slicing it in a new way, hoping to reveal something previously unseen. New procedures replaced the old, without consideration of what had previously worked or failed, and without input from me. I worked and then re-did work according to whoever was in charge at the time. Sometimes I was responsible for all of the consulting billings and payables, other times I was not, and, then, again, I was. The West Coast office prioritized our vendor payments without regard to those vendors that were critical to our operations. Our customers and vendors got confused about whom they should be dealing with and they didn't like the new tone coming from the West Coast staff. The new tone was dismissive and assumed that our vendors would be thrilled to get twenty-five cents on each dollar the Company owed them. Uncharacteristic of the years they worked with us pre-merger, they often found the Company slow to respond. I could no longer provide them with reliable information as to when or how much they would be paid. In a short time, our vendor relations were in shreds and I often heard our vendors say that they didn't recognize us anymore. Well, neither did I.

Let me give you a fairly amusing example of this new, top down, management style. At the time of the merger, I had devised a simple system for tracking the hours of the consulting and support staff and assigning those hours to consulting jobs. We used this system to track our progress on an assignment, and to measure our profitability at the end of the job. Now, consultants do not have an easy life. They are on the road a lot and are under substantial pressure to deliver their work on time to our clients. To make life as simple as possible for them and still be able to collect and assign their hours correctly I had a simple spreadsheet system that I updated once a week. This was not the most complicated system in the world, but it was minimally annoying to the consultants and I got the data I needed from them in a timely fashion. And when a consultant was swamped, he could just stand in my doorway and give the information to me verbally. While this may not work for Deloitte it was great for us.

After the merger, the interim controller required us to begin tracking consulting hours with an on-line system called Time Tiger. This was an on-line software that companies could subscribe to and use to track their consultant's billable and non-billable hours. It required a license, password, and training for each user, and was overkill for our small consulting practice. I had no input toward the decision to use Time Tiger and no one had asked any of the consultants to test the evaluation copy of this on-line software. But we were told to start using it on the following Monday. At the training class on the Friday before the Monday the comments of the consultants were that Time Tiger was too complicated and that our existing system worked just fine. I questioned why we needed to purchase licenses for each of the consultants when our existing system was, in effect, free. We were told that Time Tiger was what senior management needed to get a clear picture of the consulting practice inefficiencies and that we were to use it beginning on Monday. The level of detail desired by the interim controller was completely unnecessary for our small practice. His system took more time and effort than the savings we would likely realize in the final analysis. Well, the interim controller was replaced after three months with a new part-time controller, and Time Tiger eventually faded as part of our new reality.

Several months later the final part-time controller was replaced by COO3 whose first question was how we track the profitability and inefficiencies of the consulting staff. I offered to reincarnate the model that we had used prior to being acquired. The VP told him the Time Tiger tale and cautioned him against repeating that mistake. Instead of Time Tiger, COO3 spent sixty hours devising what some of us called irreverently the Mother of All Color-Coded Spread Sheets. It was four legal pages long and was a comparison of budgeted and actual hours for every assignment in process. Nowhere within the spreadsheet was there a calculation of profitability. The merger was a continuous source of amazement to me.

In retrospect, it is difficult for me to understand how the acquirers thought a business should be run. Had none of them ever heard of involving the employees in their decisions? Had none of them ever heard of the term "getting the employees to buy into and own a management decision?" Had they never heard of "don't reinvent the wheel?"

And then there were the small annoyances that eroded morale disproportionately more than they should have. I clearly recall the day that our postage meter was repossessed (yes, repossessed!) and we were told to buy stamps and get over it. After all, the West Coast office had been buying stamps since its inception. Of course, there was the day that our bottled water service was cancelled and we were told that if we wanted water to bring it from home. The water was followed by the cancellation of our coffee service – there was a snack shop on the ground floor of our office building that we were told to use for hot coffee. The destruction of morale was a constant chip, chip, chipping sound and became irreversible. I cannot even discuss the cancellation of the company credit card when the consultants were on the road, or the delayed payment of medical insurance that the wife of one of our consultants discovered when she took her flu ridden toddler to the doctor while her husband was traveling for the Company. Chip, chip, chip.

Simple things such as meeting payroll became an adrenaline rush. Who would get paid and when? COO3 would call me and tell me (the day before payday) that I had to inform the folks in our office, if, when and how - forget direct deposit! - they would be paid. This was something I really looked forward to, twice a month.

How could there be no money? How could finances be this awful? What had happened to the investor's capital? I truly had no answers to these questions. As matters got worse, information became scarce. Reports I once received on a weekly or monthly basis were received sporadically, if at all. Our monthly staff meetings with financial reports and progress charts ceased to be. What did I learn in the post-merger brave new world?

- Dictating change rarely works well. Avoid employee resentment by involving, to the extent possible, those who will have to implement your business decisions.

- Be an adult. If payroll is late or missed, take responsibility and conference-call the people affected and tell them.

- Respect your vendors. Remember you may need them to come through for you some day. Playing Let's-Make-A-Deal with their receivables does not amuse them.

- Above all, don't spend money to acquire a profitable company and then chip away at it until it self-destructs.

Chapter 16: Field of Screams

Contributor: Senior Consultant in the First Acquired Consulting
Practice

Narrator: The   Senior   Consultant   was   an   extremely
*knowledgeable, organized and efficient person.   He was a high
revenue generator in the consulting practice because he worked
swiftly and rarely made mistakes.   His extensive industry
experience augmented his deliberately organized work habits so
that he could deliver more work than anyone else in the consulting
practice. Senior Consultant was a jewel employee who resigned
in total disgust at his treatment by COO3 two years after the
merger with the Company.*

I came to the Company as a result of the merger of our
consulting firm with the Company. If you had told me that after
twenty-five successful years in the business world, I would be
working for people who had no clue as to what I did, or how I did
it, I would not have believed you. I would have confronted you
with, "Perhaps these folks have not done exactly the kind of work
that I am doing, but they must have done something similar." You

would have shaken your head. I would have come back at you, "Well, if they do not know what I do, or how I do it, at some point they will ask. And because they are smart people they will also ask me what tools, such as computers and data, I need to do my job." You would continue to shake your head. By now I would really be annoyed with you and I would have said, "Listen, fellow, it is impossible for the people at the top not to know the work of the Company and how that work gets done. By your definition, there would be two companies, one for those who do the work and a second for those who just come into the office. And that is not a good strategy for a successful Company." At this point I would really be wound up, and would then hit you with my unassailable logic, "No one buys a consulting practice, if they don't understand who and what they are getting. So, you tell me why they would buy us if they don't know what we do, and, by implication, don't care what we do." And you would look at me and say, "All they want is the revenue your job will generate." Me, a cash cow? Yes, after twenty-five years, I was a cash cow.

During my years of working in our industry, I have held jobs from Senior Consultant to actually managing a company with 230 employees. At the time of our merger I held the position of Senior Consultant in the consulting practice that was acquired by the Company. It is my observation and experience that the best managers motivate their employees through shared business goals. A good manager helps solve the work-problems of employees because he himself has solid, valuable experience in the industry. I will use an expression that I hate only because it is so overused, but the best managers can "talk the talk and walk the walk." And my new managers knew nothing about my job and little about our industry.

I had been working for the consulting practice for nine years, when we were acquired by the Company. At first the merger seemed like a good thing. The Company told us they had three salespeople, and I was delighted that there would finally be someone to help us sell our consulting services. Typically, in a consulting practice, the consultants are responsible for winning the assignment as well as beginning and completing the assignment. It is tough to juggle getting and doing the work, and I have handled this by doing the best work I am capable of, so that I can count on repeat work from happy clients. I am also very organized and that helps me turn out a lot of good work on time. Repeat clients are my specialty. But to have three salespeople help us with the sales process – well, it doesn't get any better than that!

The Company was presented to us, the consultants, as being technologically advanced. That, I thought, is a good thing too. We had felt for a while that our practice was losing ground against our competitors in terms of software and the whole use of technology, but this merger would, I hoped, catapult us to the front of our industry. Again, what could be better?

Also, we were told, the Company had raised money from angel investors so I assumed that the Company was well capitalized and that a whole new day was dawning.

With cautious optimism, I awaited the merger of the two firms and, according to my unassailable logic, that first Company meeting in which I was sure to be asked what I did, and what the new Company could do to make me more effective. I did not anticipate that the moment of the merger would be the peak of my sales, finance, and technology resources, or that I was to be sent out into the field to be regarded as nothing more than a cash cow. Mooo.

In order to relieve you of some of this suspense, allow me to dispel the notion that we, in professional services, ever got any assistance from the three sales guys. Nice guys, that wasn't the problem, but they were apparently focused on selling the web-based products. This was the collapse of the first of my three merger benefit assumptions – at least it died quickly in the first week's post-merger staff meeting. So, what about the financial safety net I had envisioned as well as the shower of technology?

Let me take you into my daily life as a consultant. Part of my job with the Company was conducting the field work for potential opportunities for my clients. This field work included:

- Visiting the potential site to "kick the dirt" and make a professional judgment on both good and bad site characteristics;

- Identifying competition for the proposed use for the site;

- Becoming familiar with road network patterns and translating that into positives and negatives for our clients; and;

- Visiting local planning authorities to identify planned, future, additions to the supply of direct competition in the market.

I know the idea of traveling for business sounds exciting and entertaining. You are, I hope, thinking that I fly first class with all that goes with it – free drinks and, of course, the gourmet meal. You are thinking that I stay only at five-star hotels. I have encouraged people, like my mother, to have this image, but my reality is a bit different.

Air travel has changed since 2001. More than likely I get up at 4:00am to get to the airport in time for the 6:30am flight. I stand in line, patiently I assure you, with all the "rookie tourists" to check in and get my boarding pass. (Why do rookies travel with their twelve pieces of luggage closed by rope?) The security guard and I wait, patiently I assure you, for the rookies to find their photo IDs. "Oh, did you need that? I have it packed in one of these suitcases.... was it this one?" Clearly, I travel with the only people on the planet who have not heard of September 11.

Next is the security check, where on a good day I breeze through in only twenty to thirty minutes. Since 9/11, I have had to undress, remove my shoes and belt, empty my pockets, and separate my computer from my briefcase. All while I try to balance my power breakfast (double non-fat latte and a scone) and show the security guard my photo ID and boarding pass. Of course, the alarm will still go off as I walk through the security checkpoint. Security now unpacks my luggage while the others in line, who should be waiting patiently, are anxiously watching to see where I packed the bomb this morning. No bomb being found, now I have to redress, repack, and run to my gate which will be the farthest from the security area.

Upon arrival at my destination city, I pick up my rental car and start my day. (Yes, I said start my day!) Little do I know that the Company has a surprise for me just minutes away on this particular trip.

As I try to exit the rental car lot, the attendant asked me for a valid credit card. The Corporate credit card had been turned down because the Company failed to pay their bill on time, and the attendant won't let me out of the rental car parking lot. This was not a merger benefit that I had anticipated. What happened to all of the angel investor's capital? So now it is up to me. I can either return the rental car and head back to the airport, losing a week or so in my work schedule, or I can hand over my own credit card to cover the costs of not only the rental car, but the whole field trip, because if the Corporate Card was cancelled at the car rental agency, it won't magically work at my hotel either. I hand over my personal credit card to the car rental agent and hope the Company will still be afloat and reimburse me once I return.

Upon calling the home office later in the day, I hear the real Company motto, "How does the Corporate Credit Card dare cut us off? We only missed three months payment"! And I received assurances that, of course, I will be reimbursed, once my expense report is checked, approved, and aged at the pace of fine wine. In my last six months with the Company, I was out of the office on client field trips for parts of twenty-one weeks. To maintain the schedule and deliver my work on time, it was necessary for me to complete as much work as possible in my hotel room, and on planes, with the new added pressure of never knowing if the Corporate Card was going to work. Pressure added to pressure. But my laptop saved me, and I met unbelievable deadlines.

In late winter, however, my laptop crashed taking with it all the files that had not been backed up. Luckily, I was pretty good at keeping copies of my work, so not much had to be recreated. But I had a dead, old, computer. Now I thought the miracle of the merger will kick in because these are technology people. Anticipating a state-of-the-art computer, I asked for another laptop to travel with, as my Chicago office had no additional laptops. The series of responses from the home office went from, "There are no available, extra computers" to, "Do you really need one or are you just whining?" to, "Well, we guess we could send you one of ours, but just temporarily." Please note the curious use of "ours" in the post-merger context. Keeping in mind that the majority of the billings of the Company were coming from the Chicago office, and that I was doing more traveling than anyone else, this was not the high-tech response I had hoped for.

When the computer arrived, I found that it was a back-up laptop of the Founder's and had been sitting idle in a desk drawer. While the Founder had two computers and barely knew how to use one, it was apparently okay that I was without a computer. Was it even remotely possible that the head office did not know what I did for them, how I did it, or what equipment I needed?

My new loaner computer could not be connected to our Chicago office network, nor could it run one of the critical software programs that I used on a regular basis because its operating system was old. Was this the technology bonus the merger had promised? As such, I was given an old desktop unit to connect to the Internet and printer while I was in the office. Unfortunately, this desktop unit could not run my needed statistical program and I had to resort to a *third* computer to run my essential software programs. I have always prided myself on being efficient and I have never needed to use three computers simultaneously to complete my work. My office looked like air traffic control at the O'Hare Airport.

To update my system and to get on one computer would have cost in the vicinity of $1,000, or to get a new laptop that could have handled the programs I needed would have run about $1,400. The Company, however, was having trouble meeting its payroll, so I might as well have asked for $100,000 to get updated.

I balanced those three computers on my desk for weeks but could no longer do as much field work to enhance my new position as Cash Cow. My productivity slipped and cash receipts became the focus of the weekly staff meeting. And after about a month of this silliness COO3 called and asked me how soon the Founder could have the spare computer back! They truly just didn't know how their employees did their work!

Here are the lessons that the merger with the Company taught me:

- Even though you are the ones being acquired, ask questions. If we had just asked how much investor capital was in the bank and what the budget for capital expense was, we would have had a heads-up on the ability of the merged companies to pay for necessary field work and replacement computers. Had I asked how much of their time the three sales guys were going to devote to selling professional services, I would have had a much truer picture of the post-merger situation. I would have had more realistic expectations of the merger benefits and would have been much less disappointed when nothing materialized.

- And to "Management" let me say this, hiring, elevating, and titling people who do not know your industry screams of stupidity. You can give employees titles such as, COO3, or CTO3, but those of us who do the work of your Company are not fooled. When your resources are limited, as ours were, there can be no more glaring mistake than this. Please, do not suggest that we train or teach these people. We tried and they successfully resisted us.

Have to go, they are boarding my flight!

Chapter 17: Un-Due Diligence – The Second Acquisition

Contributor: The Chief Scientist of the Second Acquired Company

---

Narrator: *Buoyed by the apparent success of the merger with the first consulting company, the Founder and the Chairman rapidly approached a small Texas software company as their second acquisition candidate. The Chief Scientist who owned the Texas company and developed its software tells here of his interaction with the Chairman and the Founder and outlines their acquisition due diligence process. The Chief Scientist was also a professor at a solid university and had lined up students who were eager to begin the development of the next version of his software. This is the tale of how the Chief Scientist accomplished just that.*

Well now, I had the Founder and the Chairman precisely where I wanted them. You see the supreme arrogance with which they approached me blinded them completely. They believed that I was a brilliant professor with no business sense because that is how I appeared intentionally. On this, the first day of their second trip to Texas to meet my employees and me, they swaggered in during the late afternoon day wearing sunglasses and smelling faintly of wine. For the occasion, I wore the same old navy blazer I had for their first visit, scuffed shoes and an old polo shirt to suggest that I might be in need of cash and open to the stated purpose of this visit which was for them to acquire my company.

I had developed a software program that was compatible, or so the Founder and the Chairman stated, with the application they had rather nicely deployed on their web site and they wanted to do what the Chairman called a "roll-up." I will explain. By this he meant that they wanted to acquire other compatible companies with compatible software to broaden their web offering. I was willing to talk with the two of them because I was seeking relief from some personal debts that were tied to my company. Also, I had plans to take my software to the next, higher level, and cash for my existing, obsolete software sounded good. My efforts to get rid of my debt and move on with my newest software concept were aided because the Founder and the Chairman actually thought they were smarter than I. How excellent.

My soft Texas accent and my vague hand gestures went a long way to convincing them that they were correct in their assumption that I was an over-educated "good ole boy," as I believe the expression goes, and they never looked much deeper than my surface. On their first visit they had asked about my sales pipeline, and on this second visit I gave them a spreadsheet that I had had a student prepare for them to review. I have often found that spreadsheets lend authority to smoke and mirrors – which the Founder and the Chairman, of all people, should have known. I became vague about the items on the spreadsheet when they asked a few easy questions, some I could answer, and some I parried because the undergraduate who had done the work was not in the office at the moment. Eventually, they moved on to ask where we should have dinner that evening.

At dinner we talked about personal things which encouraged them to think that they were getting to know me. I added no intelligence to their working knowledge of my company or me at dinner. The wine they had selected was good and at $65 a bottle it was one I might not have had an opportunity to try except for the splendid generosity of the Founder and the Chairman.

The next morning, they arrived at my office at 10:00am. They asked about my employees and I explained that I had chosen the best graduate students and Ph.D. candidates from the university to work in my company and under me. They liked the fact that I didn't have to pay these folks high salaries or benefits and the semester-to-semester employee turnover problems did not seem to register with them. Then they asked for a demonstration of my software. I had prepared for this by telling one of my students that he was going to give the demonstration and that I would be the voice-over narrator controlling the demonstration. The undergrad had agreed and we proceeded accordingly. The Founder and the Chairman smiled with approval when I explained that a student was going to help with the demo as I was, after all, the professor in charge and not an audio/visual aide. Well now, it just never occurred to them that I had not used my own software in so long that I couldn't remember how. Nevertheless, I had cleared another hurdle.

During the demonstration the Chairman, who told me he had been in the software development business for thirty years, asked several elementary questions. I kept the demonstration moving swiftly and they seemed impressed by my software and acquisition discussions resumed at lunch.

We went to a quiet steak house and when seated the Founder, who ordered a lovely pinot noir which I had enjoyed once as a dinner guest, asked me about my customer roster. I gently explained that I had focused on a market segment very different from that of the Company. They asked for client references and I gave them some client company names where I felt confident neither the Founder nor the Chairman would know anyone. They then congratulated themselves that by selecting my company as their second targeted acquisition they would be expanding into another "vertical." Allow me to simplify. This was their shorthand for saying that they had apples for customers and my customers were oranges and, instead of a conflict, they perceived this as an advantage. I restrained myself from using the apples to oranges analogy at the dining table and lunch passed smoothly.

In the afternoon, they asked about the finances of my company. I said I would have someone update our internal spreadsheet and e-mail it to them expeditiously.

Then the Founder asked me if I had any further questions. I softly mentioned that my product was software installed on computers and theirs was an application service provider, or ASP, delivered over the Internet. Was I correct, I queried, to assume that they had thought through the conversion of my product to their web delivery system and did they have the resources to accomplish this fairly complex, daunting task? The Founder and the Chairman glanced at each other and the Founder looked uncomfortable. They then explained that their technology expert, CTO3, would be calling me. I had a graduate student take that phone call.

After a bit more waltzing, the Founder and the Chairman acquired my company and software product. The Company assumed my personal debts as part of our agreement so I achieved getting out from under my personal debt burden and was welcomed back into my men's club. Unfortunately, I received no cash which was an annoyance and a personal disappointment.

Of course, there was the unpleasantness of the post-merger fuss that the Founder raised when my sales pipeline evaporated and I had to explain twice that those were sales leads not guaranteed commitments. Long distance communication with remote offices can be so trying, but these were my new working circumstances and so I was patient. There was also a good deal of unnecessary hysteria when my client references didn't pan out. Much of that work was done so long ago that the people we worked brilliantly for had moved on to other companies and were impossible to locate.

Things were tediously nasty for a while and then the Company neglected to pay me – something about my sales pipeline again. Lack of a salary forced me to have my attorney communicate to the Founder and the Chairman that they were in violation of my new employment contract. I had absolutely no choice, really. The upshot of all of this frenzy is that I have been able to start a new company and build the next version of my revolutionary software, at long last. I am free of the Founder and the Chairman, my debts and my obsolete software. How satisfactory.

Oh, yes. I have been asked to list here the lessons that I learned as a result of my association with the Founder, the Chairman, and the Company. I am sure I have demonstrated here that I taught lessons to the Company. There was really not much of any substance for me to learn from them. Therefore, no list follows.

Chapter 18: How to Create a Corporate Monster

Contributor: Saintly Operations Manager of the Acquired
Consulting Practice

*Narrator: The Saintly Operations Manager, SOM, had been
employed by the consulting practice for seven years before it was
acquired by the Company. She started with the consulting
company as a typist and quickly became the supervisor and
trainer of all the support staff of the firm, then she was promoted
to Operations Manager. In this position she efficiently oversaw the
complicated procedures of the consulting practice. There were
data and numerous fidgety, fragile, software programs to acquire
and install. There were proposals and technical reports to
proofread under countless tight deadlines, consultants to cajole
and assist, and clients with whom binding relationships had to be
formed. Salt-of-the-earth only partially describes the SOM. She
was kind, hard-working, funny, bright, and full of common sense,
all of which endeared her to her fellow workers. When she
encountered COO3, she felt as though she was dealing with an
extraterrestrial from another galaxy, and not a carbon-based
extraterrestrial, at that.*

His radioactive breath slid over the phone line and poisoned my brain through the headset. The radioactivity came alive, like a series of July 4th sparklers. On, off, on. Frizzle, silence, frizzle. Like all radiation, it mutated its subject. It turned brisk, no nonsense, straight-forward me into an irritated maniac. And COO3 did this all this remotely, over the phone, with just one call.

It was not unusual for my week to begin by making a telephone call to COO3 that would go something like this. "What I am telling you, COO3, is that I tried to open my e-mail this morning, and for the first time ever, it asked me for a password. I do not have an e-mail password. In fact, none of us in this office needs a password to get into our e-mail. This morning, however, I cannot access my e-mail, nor can anyone else in our office. What is going on, COO3?"

COO3: "Well, um, I, uh, thought — did some reading last night and set up the passwords around midnight — thought it would be prudent and smart to start using e-mail passwords. We are an Internet company after all. It can't hurt to be, uh, safe."

Me: "Please tell me what password you assigned to me, and to everyone else in this office, so we can get into our e-mail and start to work."

COO3: "Well, uh, yeah. OK. You know, all you have to do, well, just open your e-mail and change your password. No biggie."

Me: "I need the password you assigned me to open my e-mail and to change my password. What password did you assign to me?"

COO3: "Ah, yeah, um, look, I see I have another call, got to take it. Call me back."

It took me another four hours to unravel the e-mail mess. Four hours, in which we could have been productive and accomplished our work while at relative peace. But no. There were more phone calls, raised voices, and start-stop-start again. COO3 was one of the biggest professional time-sucks I had ever encountered. I will try to explain, as best I can, that period of time and, from my perspective, what happened. But, I admit, the illogic of all the things COO3 did generated a haze of negative emotions that swirled around me so that I had a very hard time not going full snap.

At the end of my employment with the Company, COO3 was the one person whom I most wanted dead. How could anybody as pathologically inept as COO3 be employable? Of course, there were many of us who theorized that COO3 wasn't really an employee of the Company. Let me start there.

About ten months after our merger with the Company, COO2 resigned and started his own computer service for small businesses. I had gotten along with COO2, but he was described to me by others who worked with him as poisonous, and I felt when he left, that it was probably good for everyone involved. We had enough to deal with without the addition of poisonous staff.

In his previous job, Future COO3 had been the sole financial advisor/analyst to a privately held fund that invested in small start-up companies. There were several criteria for a start-up company to obtain the approval of this investment fund, and the ones I recall were that the start-up company had to be in a business related to the fund's parent company, and that the start-up company had to use technology in a new way. It was Future COO3, in this former job, who recommended that his fund invest in the Company. An additional investment criterion was that someone from the fund must be placed on the Company's Board and given voting rights because of the substantial amount of the fund's investment. As it turned out, only Future COO3 had the time to sit on our Board, and to make sure he gave it his best effort, his boss required him to personally invest in the Company. His boss had said something like, "Put your money where your mouth is."

Of all of the businesses Future COO3 recommended as investments to his fund, only our Company was still operating when he was fired from the fund. This sort of limited, or focused, depending on your point of view, his next job options.

One dark, blustery, nasty, rainy morning, Future COO3 arrived at the Company's West Coast office. He explained to the Founder that as a personal investor in the Company and as an existing board member, he was going to "volunteer" his time and efforts to pull the finances of the Company into a master spreadsheet so we would know exactly where we stood. I had been involved in enough conference calls and angry, vendor phone calls to know we did not need another spreadsheet to tell us where we stood financially. We did not stand. We levitated over the corpse of our former consulting practice.

But, go figure. The Founder gave Future COO3 a cubicle followed by instructions to the interim controller who was told that he was to cooperate fully. And Future COO3 became a part of the Company. Neither an interview nor a resume was necessary because Future COO3 was a "volunteer" and not a real or paid employee. Yikes!

He did a competent job of detailing in his new spreadsheet that the Company owed a lot of money to everyone with whom it was associated. Sheesh! Now there was a surprise!

Future COO3 became very involved over the next two months explaining to anyone who would listen, such as the Founder, the Chairman and the Board, that the Company owed money to a ton of people. They, the listeners, inferred from this analysis that he was brilliant. When COO2 resigned, Future COO3 became COO3 and one of the oddest business dynamics I have ever watched was born.

Under the cloak of darkness, or so it seemed to me and everyone in our Chicago office, COO3 began to accrue power so quickly that many of us thought he was the sole reason the West Coast had had a recent energy blackout. Looking back, I think what happened was that the Founder and Chairman just dumped all the things that they were no longer interested in dealing with onto COO3, regardless of his skills, experience, knowledge or, ahem, title. In the beginning, his influence was subtle, like an annoying rash. Then, in the blink of an eye, the rash escalated into a flesh-eating disease that threatened the entire Company. He controlled just about everything, and he knew nothing about everything he controlled. So many decisions got bottlenecked by COO3 that we used to say his desk was our very own Company black hole.

Who was COO3? In short, a disastrous, unemployed, stray. Where did he come from? My answer: an unsuccessful atomic bomb test in the South Pacific.

How did he absurdly ascend to the position of COO3? The Founder wanted to off-load a lot of tiresome tasks, such as negotiating with our data vendor, "managing" the relationship with those of us in the Chicago office, digging out from under the merger with the Texas company, and untangling our relations with vendors. And there was COO3; no job, and no job description, who just said "yes" to whatever the Founder shoveled his way. Who did COO3 report to? Our guess was the Founder. Who reported to him? Honestly, no one knew.

What was his ultimate role? In my view, he accelerated the demise of the Company through his inertia. Let me explain. As time went on, COO3 just began to assume and command Co-Founder authority over everything. The E-mail password discussion with which I began this chapter became a standard operating procedure as COO3 needed to control, or at least touch, everything. Yet COO3 did not have a minute of experience in our industry nor the foggiest idea what we, the consulting practice, truly did for a living. Consequently, when we needed to buy data, he balked. When we needed a new lap-top, he stalled. When we needed the assistance of a free-lance specialist to work on an assignment, he became flustered. He could not make a decision, because he really did not know what the correct decision was. COO3's lack of industry experience was crippling us in the Chicago office and, ultimately, the Company. If I hadn't known better, and if it all had not been so serious, I would have thought COO3 was a science experiment dedicated to testing our sanity.

In fairness, every workday must have been torture for COO3 as decision after decision piled up on his desk. Why didn't he just step aside? My observation is that his ego and arrogance were fueled by those of the Founder. COO3 was unable to acknowledge his failings within the Company; and he was out of control. Perhaps, just perhaps, he was determined to make up for his failure at the previous investment fund. I sensed a bit of, "I will show you morons how to run a Company," as though he thought none of the other businesses he had the fund invest in would have gone belly up if he had been more involved in them.

Well, this gets pretty complicated, doesn't it? And I'm not done yet. Here is my last observation on the perverse, final days of the Company.

After about six months of COO3 on full power and full brakes simultaneously, the professional glue melted. Our Senior Consultant/Cash Cow resigned, the Vice President of our Chicago office got a great job offer and resigned, the ASVP and VP both resigned and enrolled in anger management classes. Who was left at the top? The Founder and COO3 (the Chairman thought he could help best by taking his second wife off to his new, custom-built home in Jackson Hole, Wyoming). This was really the end of the Company. My theory? The Founder ran off, fired, laid-off, or exiled everyone except COO3, who was the only person less competent than the Founder. The Founder ensured the Company's own failure by embracing the one person who could not help the Company and relied upon the person who knew nothing about our industry, our work, or our profession. Unbelievable, isn't it? Lessons? You bet!

- Get out of the way of employees who do the work for your Company and for you.

- Delegate tasks to appropriate employees. Identify those appropriate employees based on their skills, talents, and experience, not on their availability.

- If you are in over your head and can't make correct decisions to move the Company forward, replace yourself. You are just setting yourself up for professional failure.

- Beware of "power creep", and, as we used to say, powerful creeps. They will grind your Company to a halt. Permanently. Sheesh!!

Chapter 19: Who put the "Ass" in "Executive Assistant"?

Contributor: The Founder's Final Executive Assistant (FEA)

Narrator: *The Founder went through executive assistants as though they were cellular phones; about every eight months there was a new one. When the Final Executive Assistant (FEA) showed up for her first day at the Company, an instant betting pool was formed by the rest of the employees. How long would it take the Founder to send this perky, five-foot-one, slender, young, high-heeled, well-educated, and, they assumed, completely unsuspecting, naïve daughter-of-a-career-diplomat, screaming out the door? Two weeks were all they gave FEA. Boy, were they surprised when FEA lasted ten months, and under extremely stressful conditions. To her credit, FEA drilled some professional behavior into the Founder, at least in the beginning. Fasten your seat belts. Here are FEA's observations about Founders and CEOs.*

There is a reason they put the word "Ass" in Assistant. Ninety percent of your time as the Executive Assistant revolves around making sure the Founder does not look or act like an ass, which, in turn, makes you feel, well, like an ass.

I was hired by the Company after the two start-up companies I had previously worked for bombed. Prior to working for the Company, I had been employed as the executive assistant for a Chairman and a CEO at two different companies, both of which detonated shortly after sizzling in the venture capital tinderbox. I should have known better than to join my third start-up company, but I couldn't resist. The employment details meshed for me. First, the Company was so close to my home that the commute was a cinch. Second, the salary was good. But, third, and most important at the time, a Board member from my prior company was the Chairman of this new Company. He swore that this Company was the real deal, and I believed him because I knew, as only an executive assistant can, that he was heavily invested in the Company. Then a member of our Board recommended me for the job with the Company and actively promoted me to the Founder. I allowed the convenient location, good salary, stock options as well as outright stock grants, and a fresh start, to convince me to join the Company.

There is however, a subtext to all of this venture capital funding frenzy for those of us, the serial start-up employees, that you should know about because it is independent of salary/commute issues. We, the serial start-up employees, envision and are motivated by and are addicted to the pot-of-gold-at-the-end-of-the-rainbow probabilities that are associated with each new job and each new company we join in the venture funded world. This "it could happen to me" feeling slowly changes from a distant, vague possibility to a real expectation for serial start-up employees, and it ensnares us.

Please don't think that we are looking for something for nothing — we aren't. The work involved in forming-pushing-dragging a new company into existence overwhelms us. There is no something for nothing going on with us. Instead, we have a Big-Something-for-Everything-We-Do expectation. The Big Something is, of course, a monetary reward, disproportionately big for the amount of time, not effort, that we put into the company. This reward whoops loudly to your family and friends that you (yes, you!) were smart enough to be able to pick the winning horse out of a field of unknowns. It reflects your keen, intuitive powers and your business acumen coupled with your willingness to work like a fiend to "make it happen." Yes, the venture capital funded start-up world was like a drug for many of us.

But I was still feeling the pain of having come so close yet failing to see my prior company's stock shares go on a meteoric rise. We had been in the final stages of obtaining a mezzanine round of financing from a major Wall Street firm. This funding would have carried us until we could go public, eight months in the future. We were in the last step of this funding process: the tedious, dreaded, background checks on the principals of our company. Imagine my surprise when they discovered my CEO boss was hiding a fresh, personal bankruptcy filing. Since major Wall Street firms are reluctant to turn over $50 million to anyone with a bankruptcy, my expectations of IPO rewards went up in smoke. It made me wonder why Wall Street doesn't do background checks sooner, rather than later, in the process, but there you are.

I gathered my energies and began my job at the Company. I was the Executive Assistant to the Founder and to the Chairman, who was, you recall, a member of the Board in my previous company. I was the Assistant to both of them. It was going to be interesting to watch.

They both had many of the earmarks of Founders and Chairmen whom I had worked for previously. They both appeared to be high net-worth individuals who were well educated and had successful professional histories. (Although these credentials did nothing in my former experiences to ensure the success of those companies, I mention them anyway.) Added to these personal credentials, the Company's office was full of employees and consultants, so I assumed that something was finally going right— at least with this Company.

By the end of the first week, I was a little queasy. Had I placed myself on another sinking ship? The Founder seemed completely disconnected from the employees. The Chairman was very busy with his personal life and, I suspected, had a desk at the

Company as a reason to get out of the house rather than as a base for a serious effort to oversee the Company.

The employees appeared, from my vantage point, to be totally self-managed and self-directed. Could they be a Company within a Company; a play within a play? How Shakespearian!

I only needed to sit quietly for a moment at my desk, to feel the disdain of the employees for the Founder and the Chairman. And even more startling was the on-display disdain the Founder and the Chairman felt for their employees. In my capacity as the Executive Assistant to both the Founder and the Chairman, the employees initially treated me as though I had some deadly, contagious disease. They gave me looks of pity and avoided me in those first early weeks. But from my past start-up experiences, I knew smart and unhappy employees meant one thing: serious mismanagement at the highest levels. Here I go again?

I believe that many of the Silicon Valley venture capital funding problems at the turn of the 21st century were caused by people, like the Founder and the Chairman, suddenly having access to incomprehensible amounts of money. These people, who may have been reasonable individuals at one time, became convinced that they were superpowers because they could extract fortunes from venture capitalists. At one point, it seemed as though this money was truly infinite. It appeared that no matter how bad the decisions of senior executives were, the business itself would end up okay because the senior executives had the luxury of continuing to throw money at their bad decisions until the problem appeared fixed. What I witnessed over and over is that it becomes easy for Founders and Chairmen to lose touch with their company when money is not a problem. They do not have to worry, analyze, or assess their problems. Nor do they need to understand the skills, talents, abilities or shortcomings of their employees. They just solve the problem with money. At this point in their company's life cycle, it seems they believed that no critical thinking was required at the executive level. Just the ability to raise venture capital money.

This money-rich condition causes a critical and often lethal problem. Funding, not sales revenue generated by the company's products, becomes a safety net, and they no longer focus on product development but rather on raising the next round of funding.

When that happens, someone, usually a Board member, has to somehow get the egos of the Founder and the Chairman to snap out of their venture funding miasma and to reset their focus on new and successful product development and customer growth to push the business to succeed. But that Board member smack-down had not yet happened at the Company that I could see. The Founder was allowed to try to grow the Company through additional attempts at funding, not successful product development, and, then when that fizzled, tactics were changed and the Founder was allowed to try to "swallow" the competition.

There are, of course, problems with growth by acquisition, or accretive growth, as the venture capital world calls it. First, you the acquirer have to be smart enough and dominant enough to rid yourself of the executive management of the acquired company. Unless you do this, there will be all Chiefs and no Indians at the conference room table, no one will be smoking the peace pipe, no one will be paddling the Company canoe in the correct direction, and everyone at the top will plan an uprising to become the next Chief. The Founder never understood this.

In addition, as other businesses were added to the core Company, salary needs grew, and the overhead required to operate multiplied, and the number of remote offices exploded. The venture funding safety net had led to financial cockiness at the senior executive level, as it so often does, and suddenly the Company had more debt than income. My past experiences suggest this is often the beginning of the Demise.

The beginning of the terminal Demise of any company I work for is always my hardest professional challenge. I knew the end was coming because in my professional capacity I saw everything the Founder and Chairman did, and I was able to recognize and admit defeat long before they were. Still, I had to come to work every day with a placid look on my face, as though I were a nincompoop who couldn't see the gaping hole in the side of the canoe. This became very difficult because by this time I actually liked and respected my co-workers whom I had gotten to know.

To me, the one consistent, nasty part of Demise is always the executive management blame game. When so much of your Company business depends on programmers whose work with computers we, mere mortals, have only the most basic understanding of, it becomes easy to shift the blame onto others. The buck never seems to stop with anyone when the business is failing. Blame gets passed around like a hot potato. The Founder and the Chairman never went back to the Board or the investors with the truth: they had run the Company to the brink of destruction and now costs swamped revenues. Stating this would have been a blow to their egos.

Firmly in Demise, the Founder and the Chairman began to disappear on vacations, family events, and, when they ran out of ideas, "emergencies." As their Executive Assistant, I was left holding the bag, in many respects. I still had to take phone calls from investors, other Board members, and our attorneys and major vendors. I diplomatically explained the lack of response from the Founder and the Chairman to e-mail and voice mail messages while I tried to hold on to a bit of self-respect, phone call after call. Those who did not know me accused me of not passing their frantic messages on to my bosses. Those who knew me suspected that they might be staring into the abyss. And this went on, day after day, call after call. As I said, Demise is always a tough professional challenge for me. Based on my experience, I can state with some confidence that while the behavior patterns of the Founder and the Chairman were at the extreme end of the behavioral range, neither of them was atypical of what goes on in Demise.

Here are several professional lessons and observations that I can pass on to you from my vantage point as Executive Assistant to those at the top.

- Senior executives rarely take the blame. Today's businesses, especially those involving new ways of using technology, are so complex that very few people will actually be able to figure out what, and who, went wrong. So senior executives rarely take any blame. They blame the Information Technology (IT) group; no one can prove or disprove this, nor will they even want to try. Or, they will blame the business environment, or terrorists, or they will blame Barack Obama, or any right (or left) wing conspiracy, or their incompetent and over paid employees, or they will blame the Federal Reserve and its interest rates. You get the picture — they just never take the blame. And if they are really inept and somehow they get caught and they are forced to take some of the blame, they will claim they are having marital/health/family/depression problems. These problems are currently on the understandable-personal-issues list. These issues act as criticism deflectors to ensure senior executives that future employment will be attainable. Tip: Before using any of the understandable-personal-issues, check with your Executive Assistant because the issues list changes swiftly, illogically, and irrevocably.

- Business plans are written over and over and, somehow, no one completes this critical document. As the Executive Assistant, I was the keeper, or the locator, of the Business Plan and, as such, was an indispensable person. I knew what, who, how and when the latest (never final) version of the Business Plan came to be. Most importantly, I knew where it was saved on the computer network, and I could access it in an instant. Tip: Executive Assistants should keep the Business Plan out of their boss's hands. In the hands of your boss, it means endless hours of meaningless revisions. (I have often wondered why the Business Plan is imbued with such sacred power yet is constantly revised. Shouldn't it be a well thought out plan instead of taking on the appearance of senior level busy work? Just asking.)

- Senior executives rarely hesitate to acquire or merge with another company when a decisive action is required as a diversion or cover for yet another failed quarter. The financial condition of the to-be-acquired company seldom matters. In fact, if the acquisition target is financially weak, the acquiring senior executives will present themselves as the more powerful of the two entities and will issue a news release with well-constructed quotes stating the combination of two, (weak), companies will now revolutionize the world. Tip: Use acquisition to rid yourself of employees whom you don't like by calling them redundant even if you have no idea what they do for your Company.

- To avoid any tough decisions, senior executives often require a full week of "travel," and if they work this right, the problem will go away (quit), disappear, (be solved by whoever fills in for them), or will be eclipsed by another issue which can be lobbed elsewhere in the Company. Tip: Senior Executives can deal more easily with anything if they have a fabulous tan.

- As this chapter was written, e-mail was an "emerging" technology for many senior executives. By emerging I mean few executives have emerged from their caves to know how to use it effectively. This is a clever and deliberate senior executive ruse. When the senior executives do not know the answer to an e-mail query, they have their Executive Assistant respond with an e-mail that answers an unrelated question, ignoring the topic at hand. The Executive Assistant looks like, well, an ass, but this tactic often succeeds in disheartening the sender of the original e-mail. Tip: Senior executives should instruct their Executive Assistants to send any pesky, impertinent, annoying questions to the employee who will be able to answer them. The proper employee will answer the e-mail, and the problem will be resolved.

- As a person who has participated, on occasion, in the Demise until the very end, I am still amazed at the sheep-like behavior of some employees. If you don't pay them, but you promise to pay them, some employees will still come to work. Give them a vague, approximate pay day, and some employees will work even harder for fear of losing their jobs and their now accrued salary. Tip: When you go out of business and close the doors, senior executives must be vigilant and send home those employees who still tend to show up at the office because they believed in the business premise.

Oh, well, I still wish the Company had succeeded, but I am on to my next business challenge!

Chapter 20: Balancing Act

Contributor: The Part-time Bookkeeper

> **Narrator:** *The Part-time Bookkeeper, PTB, was the second employee hired by the Founder and just about the last one to leave the Company. Even though she saw the lifecycle of the Company through part-time glasses, she suffered her fair share of stress because the chronic, poor, cash flow of the Company meant she had to juggle angry vendors and their accounts payable on a weekly basis. She was intensely loyal to the Founder and viewed the internal workings of the Company in a different light than most of the other employees.*

I am a student of Buddhism and I truly believe that the universe gives us back what we put out into it. I believe that positive karma is necessary for a peaceful, spiritual, and productive life. I have a growing, therapeutic massage practice and my avocations are yoga and spiritual development. I am writing this chapter in defense of the Founder, even though my spiritual advisor has told me to work on detachment which is the hardest of all the Buddhist practices, because there were several main problems with every single person who was employed by the Founder.

First, none of the Company's employees ever understood how frustrating this must have been for the Founder and the Chairman. It makes you understand that when they took refuge by ignoring the employees that the Founder and Chairman were just trying to deflect criticism and protect themselves. Keep in mind, the business concept that the employees were to implement was that of the Founder, who had put a chunk of personal fortune into the Company. The Founder and the Chairman made hard decisions the best they could and none of the employees ever got these simple facts. The employees were there to bring to fruition the Founder's dreams, not the other way around. Why should the Founder, and to a lesser degree the Chairman, have to listen to any employee? It wasn't the employee's Company and, I believe, the Founder and the Chairman were entitled to run the Company the way they thought best.

Another thing that the employees never fully understood was that the Company was a start-up Company. There is a lot of risk in joining a start-up Company and the Founder's money was at stake. A start-up Company is full of uncertainty and if you don't have the stomach for late paychecks or partial paychecks or stock-for-pay or un-reimbursed travel expenses, then go work for Microsoft. I really mean this. If you are a vendor who sells goods or services to start-up companies, then be aware of the risks which are inherent in the nature of start-ups and recognize that from time to time you may have to accept late payments, partial payments, or twenty-five cents on the dollar. And, please, stop complaining and being negative when these start-up type things happen because that sends negative energy into the universe that will come back to haunt you. All I am saying is don't blame the start-up for acting like a start-up, for goodness sake.

I had a good relationship with the Founder because I understood that it was, indeed, not my Company and I supported the Founder fully. I met the Founder through a man I was dating who was the Founder's personal fitness trainer. He told me some amusing stories about the Founder's gym behavior that made me curious. For example, the Founder liked using the cell phone while on the tread mill. Often, my boyfriend said, the Founder would edit the business plan or a contract while on the tread mill because otherwise "treading" could be seen as a waste of executive time. I admired that kind of multi-tasking devotion to the job and Company. One day, after my 60-minute yoga class, my boyfriend introduced me to the Founder because the Company needed an accountant. The Founder together with the Chairman interviewed me in the health club juice/smoothie/tea bar because their commitment to the Company was so strong they did not want to waste time.

There were several issues that needed to be worked out before I took the job offer. The salary they offered me was too low, when I calculated it on an hourly basis, for me to become a full-time employee, as the Founder wanted. Accounting was not my first love as a profession, massage therapy was, and I felt that if I was going to spend a lot of time as an accountant that I needed extra compensation to make it worth my while. I also had to gently tell them that I would always be there for the Company, but that I needed a flexible schedule. I am not the kind of person who can accept a 40-hour work-week. Once I explained that I had a lucrative, personal massage business and many regular clients, they began to understand my need for a flexible schedule. We talked at length about the hands-on healing that can come through massage and the importance of stress relief and inner peace in today's hectic world. We also discussed the importance of exercise and healthy, organic, toxin-free foods and the role of soy in today's diet. I remember all of this because yoga, diet, and inner growth toward spiritual peace were goals for me and I was pleased that they shared them with me.

I negotiated a part-time, lucrative, flexible schedule that accommodated my private massage clients and my workout schedule and I accepted the Founder's job offer.

The early days were exciting. I juggled the Accounts Payable and Accounts Receivable (AP/AR) as well as the payroll. We grew and added employees and then the Founder's role shifted to fund raising. The Founder was absolutely brilliant at this aspect of the job and was successful in attracting the interest of angel investors. Angels are wealthy individuals who invest their personal money in a start-up company. The Founder convinced a medium-size club of twenty-two angel investors to invest in the

Company. We desperately needed the cash inflow as I was exhausted from the number of angry vendor phone calls I had to field. When the angel's money came on board, I proudly told the other employees that the Founder had saved them. It was a personal vexation that I would have to process twenty-two sets of paperwork because they invested as individuals not as one club. Once I pointed out to the Founder that, of course, I was there for the Company, but that this extra workload was a strain, I was able to hire a part-time accountant to help with the AP/AR aspect of my job. The Founder was a completely empathetic, understanding boss, but why didn't the other employees see it?

I noted over time that there was a clear, predictable, pattern to the behavior of the Company's employees. They would join the Company full of energy and enthusiasm. Sleeves would get rolled up and work would get done. As time passed, however, every single employee began to feel a truly inappropriate sense of, how shall I phrase it, "ownership" in the Company. Partly, it was because the Founder had granted them all, even part-time me, stock options that vested over time, so in that narrow sense the employees were "owners". The Founder intended these stock options to make up for the less-than-market-rate salary that the Company was forced to pay the employees because of the erratic cash flow of the Company. Now, the Company did not have to do this, but it generously did, and the employees never understood how benevolent the Founder and the Chairman were. When this inappropriate employee "ownership" feeling kicked in, I could predict exactly what would happen. The employee would offer the Founder advice on a current job issue and it would always be from the employee's perspective, never from the Founder's perspective. They never understood that their prior job experience was just not interesting to the Founder and that the Founder truly felt it was irrelevant. When ignored, the employee would generate a dark energy, instead of a positive energy. None of them ever understood that they were draining the Company and the Founder. How did the Company attract the most immature people on this planet?

Well, over the life of the Company, cash flow was always an issue but I did the best I could. When the Founder acquired the first consulting practice, the cash flow from their clients went a long way toward paying our vendors. I had to become creative about dealing with health insurance and Company credit card payments, but this new set of employees from the acquired consultancy raised whining to an art form. Occasionally, I had to let some payment dates slip and the Company credit card, for example, would be frozen by the credit card company. Over and over again, I would patiently explain to the consultants who were on the road that cash was tight, yes, the credit card had been frozen again, and that they needed to be flexible. This was something the consultants never understood and was always a puzzle to me. Didn't they know that they had been acquired by a start-up company? Frankly, they howled as much or worse than our outside vendors did. It was clear to me that unless the consultants got more efficient and could generate more income, the Founder and I were always going to have to juggle payments. The consultants did not understand this basic fact of life and their stress increased.

The Founder's second acquisition was a perfect example of how the employees consistently took advantage of the Company. The Founder and the Chairman acquired a Texas company whose software was to be used to streamline the work of our unreasonable consultants as the software itself was transitioned into a new web-based product for the Company. First of all, when the consultants were shown the software after the acquisition closed, they claimed it would not automate any of their work effectively. (Keep in mind, they still wanted paychecks on time!) Then I discovered that the second acquired company had debts that were not revealed prior to the Founder's acquisition of the company and their sales pipeline turned out to be hot air – not a single new client ever signed up! Of course, the typical, habitual, internal carping began and not a single employee saw it from the Founder's perspective. The Founder's hands were tied by this second acquisition to push the Company forward and all we needed was a little cooperation from Company employees so the Founder could do what was best.

I was grateful that I had my massage clients, my yoga, and my meditation during this time because protecting the Founder from difficult employees was stressful.

Things ended in a fairly typical manner for many start-up companies. After four-years with the Founder, I was asked to work fewer hours for less salary. Of course, this was impossible for me to do financially. I got several, new, massage referrals and told the Founder that I was not spiritually abandoning the Company, rather, I just was just physically moving on. We still talk once a week and I will believe forever that the Founder was the most misunderstood person who ever tried to grow a business. And all by the employees who were supposed to be working for the Company! Here are the lessons I want to leave with you:

- Exercise and diet can be very helpful in getting you through super-stressful situations such as the one I witnessed at the Company.

- Meditation and yoga can be used to alleviate stress. Controlling your thoughts allows the stress to flow around you – you do not have to get caught up in it. Getting control over your emotions is important.

- You do not have to absorb the anger of unreasonable people, just let it flow around you and back to them.

The universe gives back to you what you put out into it. Be peace!

Chapter 21: Scenic Overlook – The Investor's View

Speaker: Investor and Board Member (IBM)

Narrator: A personal investor in the Company who subsequently became a Board Member agreed to be interviewed to share his view of the Company from the top. The company he spent his career with was well run and the darling of Wall Street. When he retired, the stock price was near its historic high. He had a large, if undiversified, investment portfolio and was advised to attend to its diversification. He did this by investing in the Founder's Company. He reveals his honest opinions about the Board and Board meetings. He acknowledges the Founder's chaos and reluctantly accepts any responsibility for the Company crisis. He also gives his interesting take on the Founder's forceful, fatal personality.

Narrator: Why did you personally invest in the Company?

IBM: Yes, well, let's start at the beginning. I had been the senior vice president of a large, successful company for twenty-five years before retiring. The Founder made a sales call to me before I retired and showed me the web-based products the Company was developing. My company spent over $3 million a year in the kind of research that they were attempting to do on-line. We could not use their service because of our own internal politics, yet I was impressed because I believed that the products were very right for our industry. In fact, I knew they were. The Founder's sales pitch stayed in my mind and I was intrigued with the concept. Soon after, I retired and the Founder convinced me that I should personally invest in the Company. I agreed because I believed the Founder could raise the money the Company needed for the long haul and, again, I believed the products were right for our industry. I needed to diversify my own portfolio and wanted to invest in young companies that spoke to our industry in new ways. The Founder's Company fit my start-up company investment philosophy.

Narrator: How much did you invest in the Founder's Company?

IBM: $500,000.

Narrator: All at once?

IBM: No, in two steps. My first investment was $250,000. Then four months later the Founder came back to me and I added $250,000 to my initial investment. Let me say that at the time $500,000 bought less than 7% of the Company and I felt comfortable that the risk was shared among all the investors. I knew and admired several of the other personal investors and felt with our shared industry experience we were good resources for the Founder. As general advisors, we brought more than capital to the Company; we brought experience and guidance to the table.

Narrator: What was the second $250,000 used for so soon after the first investment?

IBM: The Chairman and the Founder wanted to acquire a consulting practice and they needed additional funding for that acquisition.

Narrator: What was your opinion of this acquisition?

IBM: I felt it was a sound business decision because the cross-selling opportunities were substantial. Once acquired, the consultants could sell the Founder's web-based products to their clients and the Founder could conversely sell the consulting services to the Company's web-based customers. At least, it made sense when the Founder and the Chairman pitched it to me.

Narrator: How did you land on the Board of the Company?

IBM: With my second $250,000 investment, the Founder and the Chairman asked me to become a Board Member. They said they needed my expertise and I agreed to join the Board. There was a not-so-hidden-agenda in this request. The Founder really wanted my industry contacts to help the Company sell both the web-based products and the consulting services. I often found myself uncomfortable with their level of sales aggression, but that is not germane to this conversation.

Narrator: Describe an average Company Board Meeting.

IBM: Sorry, I will try to stop smiling but I was afraid that you were going to ask me that. Let me just say that all of the board meetings were run by the Founder who composed the agenda and back-up materials. In every meeting the agenda was different, the pace of the conversations differed, and all the back-up materials were poorly presented. With other Boards on which I have served, the agendas were driven by the needs of the business rather than the agenda of the founder and the back-up materials arrive in plenty of time for participants to study them and pencil in appropriate questions. The Founder's materials arrived so late that I always felt unprepared for the meeting, as did the other members. After several meetings, I felt that the purpose of the fast pace of the topics was intended to keep us, the board members, in the dark.

Narrator: Did you ever try to add an item to the agenda?

IBM: I was never asked if I wanted to add anything to the agenda.

Narrator: But, not being asked aside, did you ever try to add a topic to the agenda?

IBM: The Founder did not want any tough questions.

Narrator: Did the Founder report to the Chairman of the Board?

IBM: Yes, of course. The Chairman complained to the Founder and to the Board in general on several occasions about the late delivery of back-up materials and the unprofessional way the meetings were run. But his comments and complaints fell on deaf ears. The Founder deflected negative comments and the meetings eventually just perpetuated themselves. The Chairman expected his criticisms to generate corrective actions which never materialized.

Narrator: The Founder deliberately misread or just ignored the instructions of the Chairman, and the Chairman allowed this? Then in your opinion, was the Chairman serious about his relationship with the Company?

IBM: I believe that the Chairman and the Founder had a different agenda from the rest of the Board. I believe that short and long-term goals should work together, short term goals getting you to the long-term ones successfully. The Founder and the Chairman just focused on one long-term goal – to whom could they sell the Company?

Narrator: The business plan had a sales revenue goal of $400 million in the fifth year...

IBM: Yes, I know that was what they had on paper but I never believed in the business plan. Instead, I believed in the product concept.

Narrator: Did they have a serious plan to get to the $400 million? After all, their sales revenue never went above $2.2 million.

IBM: No, the business plan was a marketing tool they used to raise funds. The sole intent of the Founder was to build the web-based products and then sell the Company.

Narrator: Board meeting after Board meeting, you all tolerated a manipulated agenda and late meeting materials. The Founder rejected guidance meeting after meeting, sales goals went unmet and no one was held responsible. Why didn't someone say to the Founder, "Sit down, stop talking, and here is what we expect at these meetings from now on?" Why didn't the Board mutiny?

IBM: The Board was composed of very wealthy individuals. None of our personal investments in the Company amounted to a significant percent of our portfolios. Our investments were not what any of us would consider huge or, to put it another way, serious. No one wanted to spend the energy to make the appropriate changes to the leadership of the Company, and the energy we would have needed to apply to affect change would have had to huge and applied constantly in every phone call, e-mail, and board meeting with the Founder.

Narrator: The Company had employees and customers and shareholders and vendors. Why didn't the Board feel any fiduciary responsibility to them?

IBM: I, for one, assumed that the Chairman was more involved in the business than he was. After all, he had years of experience growing and taking his own company public. He had a reassuring and proper level of experience for the Company. In retrospect, I put my investment in the wrong hands. Yes, it is fair to say that the Board meetings were a carefully orchestrated but horribly executed performance.

Narrator: Why didn't you just resign from the Board?

IBM: I did resign, but the Founder persuaded me to stay.

Narrator: Wait a minute. You have said the Board meetings were an amateur production, that complaints were made to the Founder by the Chairman yet nothing changed, and each meeting was a misery. Yet, you allowed yourself to be talked into staying on the Board?

IBM: I guess I am more easily manipulated than I thought. I am embarrassed to tell you that I increased my involvement with the Company instead of decreasing it.

Narrator: Well, this should be interesting. Did you feel that the Founder took advantage of your experience and retirement?

IBM: Yes, the Founder and Chairman argued that since I was having problems with the way the Company was operating that I should join the Company to help out. They said that they had no money to pay me, of course, but that I should come out of retirement and help. And I joined three days a week. I actually commuted 63 miles a day to work for the Company. Being in the office and participating in various meetings was unsettling because I saw how truly dysfunctional the Company was

Narrator: What did you find?

IBM: First, the Founder painted a rosy picture to the Board but, when I had the chance to join in sales demonstrations and in sales meetings, I discovered that many potential sales were just figments of imagination. Second, at every Board meeting strategic alliances were dangled in front of us - all of which were with large, established companies that could have propelled the Company forward but, I found out, these deals were not even close to being consummated. Third, I heard call after call and saw in meeting after meeting that the Founder was always negotiating and always trying to work an angle. Nothing was straightforward business. It exhausted me to try to keep track of it.

Narrator: Did you try to do anything about the mess?

IBM: I went so far as to encourage the Board to insist that the ASVP be made the President and responsible for daily operations of the Company. But even with the Board vote and title changes, the Founder didn't relent. The vote of the Board to replace the Founder was literally ignored. When the Board spoke in one voice to the Founder our responsibilities and professional suggestions were simply ignored.

Narrator: From the employee's point of view, the Board must have appeared disinterested.

IBM: Perhaps that it how they interpreted what might have looked like the passivity of the Board. But you have no idea the strength of the Founder's will which was not only persuasive and convincing; it was relentless. I had to gather all of my strength for any simple interaction with the Founder, let alone a confrontation. Since this is anonymous, I will confess that every Board member was intimidated by the Founder. The Board ended up just going through the motions, meeting after meeting. We gave plenty of professional advice, none of it was ever taken and we became as demoralized as the employees of the Company.

Narrator: Was there any private discussion among the Board members about telling the Founder to exit the Company?

IBM: The Board realized the seriousness of the "Founder" problem woefully late. There was no money to hire a new, experienced CEO to turn the Company around, and that ended the conversation. Well, truthfully, there was a general feeling that the Founder was, after all, the original investor who had thought up the concept that the Company was created for. There were conversations among the Board members; half of whom felt we needed to respect the Founder's ownership and the other half thought we needed to "save" the Company from the Founder. In the end, the Board wound up agreeing that we did not want to place our collective will and energy up against the Founder, only to ultimately lose.

Narrator: The Company, its employees, and the concept were doomed?

IBM: Yes, and I have returned to peaceful retirement.

Chapter 22: "So, How was Your Day, Dear?"

Contributor: The Husband of the Vice President

Narrator: The husband of the VP watched hopefully, then warily and then in despair as the Company failed to achieve its potential and headed toward disaster. The VP's husband is a partner in his own business and saw the Founder of the Company commit management errors the likes of which he had never witnessed in his long career. He watched, helplessly, as his wife and her co-workers were unable to overcome the damage inflicted by Senior Management. The Company had a great business concept and the husband was amazed at the quality of the Company customer roster. It should have worked.

I am very proud of what my wife, who was the VP, and her colleagues accomplished at the Company. I don't think anyone in or out of their industry will ever fully appreciate the thinking, the ideas, and the miracle products that these genuinely and exceptionally good people produced in such a short time. This book is evidence of the creative collaboration that the employees shared and of which they were capable. From my point of view, it should have worked and, for a while, it did.

This Company fit my wife's job ideals in her quest to be part of a successful start-up. Her job involved the creation of a much-needed product by using a new technology and, of course they were up against an unrealistic deadline. This was my wife's definition of a "challenge." She accepted the position of VP knowing that she was entering uncharted waters. But it was the challenge of it all that got her toes tapping and her enthusiasm for problem solving charged up. I can recall the early days when she would come home with high anxiety over whether she was capable of integrating her exceptional industry knowledge with a new technology; or better yet, whether she was going to be able to get the software engineers to understand that the product mattered as much as the technology that was to drive it.

I manage a successful, small professional service business, and I know first-hand the pressures of attracting good talent, forming a sales strategy, meeting payroll, and just generally running a company in which people want to work. I watched my wife's Company evolve and dissolve several times over the dinner table for more than four years.

She had high hopes, as did others in the Company, that if successful in this data/technology integration, they would have a sure industry winner and that going public would bring riches to all. Dreams of valuable stock options danced in their heads. It is curious how a dream with great potential for success can become a stark, failed reality due to an uninspired Board of Directors, plus a misguided, dysfunctional Founder, and the arrogance and stupidity of a few key people who squelched both new ideas and creative employees.

It was a constant battle on several fronts: product vs. technology; teamwork vs. the individual; focused vs. scatterbrained behavior. I witnessed these battles through my wife's eyes as her emotions swayed between excitement at making a breakthrough with the product, and disgust in confronting a roadblock formed by the very people who were supposed to move the Company forward. It was indeed a motley crew and reminded me of O'Toole's book, *A Confederacy of Dunces*. How could one expect to launch a new web-based product with employees and special consultants scattered around the country, each with different agendas and different visions as to the purpose of their efforts? How could they develop an easy-to-use web interface, acquire a secure, accurate data base, wow customers with the web-based products, discover and implement that perfect product, and get status names on the Board as investors while in a scattered, hysterical environment? Of course, it drove my wife crazy when the Chief Engineer made business decisions for the Company and made them incorrectly. While she felt responsible for this waste, the real shame was that no one was held accountable for it.

In looking at it from the outside, it is a miracle that the web-based products and technology actually gelled. A lot of brainpower was transmitted across the country, and bonds were made amongst a cadre of company soldiers who saw the light of the Founder's vision and kept the vision alive. Yes, many prayers were said (most of which were, "Dear Lord, let me keep my sanity") and many prayers were answered ("Thank you, Lord, this paycheck is on time"). What kept my wife going as VP was that she had unshakable faith in the products they were building and believed in the Internet as a revolutionary product delivery system.

But faith alone can carry you only so far if the company does not have a seasoned sales team to market the product upon launch. I remember vividly the day my wife came home to tell me the exciting news that, after months of testing, the products had successfully passed the beta test period, but to then tell me over dinner that she and CTO2 had turned to pass the baton to the sales team only to see the baton fall to the floor. There was no sales team; there was only a single salesman. How was it possible that there was no trained sales team when the Company's viability and potential for additional investment dollars depended on having a product to sell and having a marketing strategy to sell the product? This was a classic case of business mismanagement.

Fortunately, there were sufficient moments of hilarity and silliness to keep the sane from going off the deep end. It was perhaps some of these giddy moments that kept my wife from going berserk. For example, there were the in-house acronyms, i.e. WATCO, "We Are a Technology Company" that they created the day the printers, fax, and email didn't work. Their financial escapades always amazed me, too.   In the face of their own insolvency, there was the purchase/merger of not one, but two, companies which necessitated a Company name change one week prior to the launching of their new products at the year's major trade show.

The astounding personal escapades never quit either. At the same trade show for their main product launch, the Founder broke a foot while dancing and my wife and the EVP had to cover all of the Founder's appointments for the remaining two days.

It seemed to me, from my perspective as a small business owner, that the personnel escapades were ridiculous and preventable.   There was, for example, the outrageous moonlighting job of the Chief Engineer in the Utah office which abused, in my opinion, the trust of the Founder and the other employees.   That fellow got fired twice, if I remember correctly.   And then the employees were abused when they fell for the Founder's stock-instead-of-pay shell game (where is the money)?   I frequently and not so silently referred to the Company as Mindwalk.com.

In the end, which to my amazement didn't happen sooner, the Company succeeded in garnering a customer base that read like a Who's Who in their industry. One can measure success in many ways: financial reward, fame, or share of market.   Even though the Company did not succeed in all of these areas it did succeed wonderfully in developing an integrated, web-based product that produced "wows" from customers.   It should have been an enormous success, but it was a professional and personal disaster. In the end, my wife equated the Company with herself and began to feel that the Company's failure was her failure. "Not so," say I, the husband.

Lessons for the VP: In hindsight, one can always produce a litany of what went wrong and, as a spouse, one can always say: "I told you so". But at the same time, the reality is that hindsight and husbands can shed some light on things gone awry. I am a Virgo, and you may know we pay close attention to detail, so let me list the lessons from my perspective.

Listen to your spouse. He or she knows you better than most other people and can not only sense the change in you when things are not right and when your work is controlling your life, but can also see it in your eyes, in your frown, in your new mannerisms (finger nail biting), in your short fuse, in your loss of humor, and in your loss of health. A spouse is not, necessarily, a genius and does not always know best, but a spouse does know when something is wrong. Listen when we struggle to help you make sense of it all.

You are more important than the Company. Do not lose sight of the fact that the Company, especially a small company, relies on the creative energy that flows through the organization and that you are a valuable contributor to the energy. But more importantly, do not forget that the company does not own you, and your self-worth is more valuable than the company's absurd demands on your time, your psyche, your family, your health, your free time, and your spirit.

Learn to say no. There came a time in the death spiral of the Company's management hierarchy when my wife was pressed to take on the simultaneous roles of Sales Director and Customer Service Director. Knowing the desperate need of the Company to increase sales, she threw her heart and soul into giving the sales effort structure and focus, meanwhile still trying to keep her primary job, Product Development, alive and the customers happy. She shook up the sales team and got them believing in the products and the importance of "closing the deal". For once, it was beginning to resemble a real company with a real sales force. Ten weeks later Founder and the Chairman declared that my wife was no longer in charge of Sales. The Founder had raised sufficient money for the second company acquisition and had nothing else to do, so the Sales function went back to the Founder. Learn to say no to stupid managers who demand impossible results and then, when you get those results, ignore them.

Know when to hold them; know when to fold them. This job was an investment and a gamble and there is nothing wrong with that. It was a tremendous investment of time and energy on the part of many employees (not to mention the financial commitment of the angel investors) and a gamble by all the employees that it would pay off. As the line from the song suggests, you collectively need to know when it is time to call it quits and switch from start-up to shut down. The Company kept on going long after it should because the Founder and several others at the top earned "accrued" salary. Accrued salary means you get the promise of a pay check but no real pay check – and these wealthy individuals could do this indefinitely. Well, going to work and not getting paid for over a year is what I call Failure Denial. In any other company, people work and they get paid. If they don't get paid, the Company folds. But here, individual wealth meant not having to face up to closing the Company. As an employee, there is a time to stop, and move on with the rest of your life.

Technology does not replace good ideas or good thinking. True, this was a web-based product that needed technology to drive it, but without the ideas and thinking of the business people who developed the product concept, the technology had no purpose. The "idea" people need a framework within which to brainstorm and explore product possibilities just as much as "technology" people need hardware and software to increase their efficiency and productivity. There must be a collaborative, synergistic, respectful, relationship between the two groups.

Life is real. *Life is real, life is earnest, and the grave is not its goal; dust thou art to dust returneth, was not spoken of the soul.* (Henry Wadsworth Longfellow). This quote should have a real meaning for the individual caught up in the chase and in the quagmire of a mismanaged company----don't lose your soul trying to make yourself and other people rich.

Lessons for the Spouse: I must confess, I learned many lessons during this endeavor.

Lesson One is never say, "I told you so". Not only does this show that you are insensitive to your spouse's plight, but it also expresses the feeling that you do not believe the efforts your spouse is attempting will work.

This leads to **Lesson Two:** Be patient. The established business world you may live in produces new products, reports, and projects on a daily basis; but a start-up company needs time to discover its real mission and the methodology that can achieve it. You may think it happens overnight but be patient and reflect that attitude in your tone and questions.

This brings us to **Lesson Three:** Give your spouse all the positive support you can. Cook fried eggs for breakfast; offer praise for a job well done; take your spouse out to dinner to unwind. Try to put yourself in your spouse's shoes. Figuratively, anyway.

Lesson Four: Imagine what it is like to work day in and day out for a misguided group of Senior Managers. Again, walk a mile in your spouse's (figurative) shoes. God forbid, but this could happen to you.

This was a very stressful job for my wife, and in an interesting way, it forced her to seek unusual outlets to relieve her stress which have subsequently brought her much solace. If there is some benefit or silver lining to such a grueling, thankless endeavor, she learned to make time for gardening and some fly fishing. Perhaps initially these activities were used as an escape, but now these tasks are joyful and have helped develop my wife into a more well-rounded, figuratively speaking, human being.

Chapter 23: Lights-Out, Life Lessons

First Contributor: Vice President (VP)

I came to write my half of this final chapter in a circuitous way, but since you have read this far, please stick with me. In this chapter, ASVP and I depict personal and professional perspectives about what we learned from our experience with the Company. I clearly have many individual lessons to mull over during my retirement (I may write a book), but there has been one gigantic, overriding lesson for me that can be explained only in the following way.

CTO2 loved anecdotes, and he used a lot of them to illustrate his numerous, but often good, points. The one that nagged at me most is the anecdote that I thought was his worst, goofiest, and dumbest. You may recall the tale of the frog in a pot of room-temperature water, and how the heat under the pot was increased very slowly, degree by degree, until the water reached the boiling point. But because the water was heated so slowly, the frog did not notice until it was too late to escape. That is truly an aggravating tale for me; how stupid can a frog be? How insensitive to environment, work or otherwise, can a frog / person be and not notice that the path they are on is deadly? How blind can the frog be that it cannot see, regardless of all the vigorous, dedicated, serious, persistent swimming around, that it is not finding cooler water? How ignorant can the frog be that it does not understand that it exists in a toxic environment and is doomed to failure? In hindsight, I was that stupid frog, and that really annoys me. Here are some lessons of life that I am eager to pass on:

- **Don't be afraid to invest in your business dream.** There are individuals who have fulfilled their life's professional dream and, if they invest in your company, it is because they want you to succeed. These investors are patient, and they are also on your side because they know, that without successful dreams, the world makes no progress. They also know that even failed dreams push the world forward because something has been learned from the attempt; however, they prefer success! They invest their money, and it is up to you to invest your time, energy, talent and make every effort to succeed.

- **But don't get lost in your business dream.** Take a stark, brutally honest look at your work environment, and force yourself to make a conscious reality judgment about it. Is yours a treacherous environment or a strong, supportive one? Is the company strategy clear? Is everyone focused on rowing the canoe in the same direction? Unfortunately, our Company's strategy changed every week. Ask yourself, are job descriptions clear, or is everyone allowed to go his own way with no accountability or supervision? Such a frivolous and undisciplined work place can lead only to failure

- **One definition of insanity is trying the same thing repeatedly hoping for a different outcome.** Some people cannot or will not change, and this must be acknowledged so that you do not persist in believing that people will get better. Things probably won't get better, and after you give it your best shot, take your talent, energy, and skills, and move on.

- **All things are possible with persistence.** Persistence is important to distinguish from the description of "insanity", above. You try, you fail, you evaluate, and try again, but differently. This is persistence, not insanity, because you learn from your evaluations, and proceed differently.

- **When someone tells you something you think is unbelievable, believe him.** I did not believe the Chairman when he decided, after two successful product launches, that we were to stop developing our unfinished product. CTO2, however, did believe the Chairman, and resigned two weeks later. I continued in the Company for an additional two years, sure that sooner or later the Chairman would waken and reverse the unbelievably bad decision he had made. This is an important lesson, so let's dissect what really went wrong. CTO2 listened to, and believed the Chairman when he made an illogical, potentially disastrous business decision. But CTO2 was wise enough to know the Chairman was working from an irrational emotion that no one else could understand, and CTO2 prudently removed himself. I, on the other hand, "knew" the Chairman would change his mind. Note here that I didn't hope, suspect, or wish; rather, I "knew." Do not assume that your reasoning and logic will ultimately prevail. There is an excellent chance that they won't. People work from different motivations, and some of those motivations may be so far removed from yours that those people appear to reside in a parallel universe. Therefore, do not become so immersed in your work waiting for a Chairman to change his mind that you permit two years to pass.

- **When someone tells you something that sounds believable, question it.** This is the skill of separating spin or hype from results. Do the person's words match his actions, and does the person get results? Listen to what is said and compare what is said to what is accomplished. We had, at one point, six potential acquirers for the Company, and at staff meeting after staff meeting these prospects evaporated. Did any one of us ask how many of the six potential acquirers were coming to our office for their due diligence effort? No one asked. Keep in mind that not all sales, strategic alliances, or deals close successfully, but if your company comes up empty in situations like these, time after time, you must question what you are being told by senior management and you must force yourself to see the nothingness that they are producing. The carrot of a potential buyer for the Company was held out at staff meeting after staff meeting so that employees would continue to work hard for a bright future, a future that never materialized.

- **Bright, creative, hardworking employees that pull together as a team can produce spectacular results that will not necessarily result in a successful company.** If there are serious, fundamental problems with the business decisions of the senior management, and if the Board of Directors does not see, acknowledge, or act to correct these problems, then the employee's efforts and the investor's capital will all be wasted. In the end, software and a handful of great clients were all that was left of the Company. In two years, the thirty plus-year-old consulting practice the Company had acquired was decimated. The software development team was reduced to a maintenance mode just to keep the servers plugged in for our remaining clients. No matter how hardworking, bright, and creative employees may be, someone at the top must see the

Company clearly and make wise, even sometimes painful decisions for the sake of investors and faithful customers.

But there was a good lesson, too. Even in the advanced years of your career, you can find a job that pushes you to apply your professional experience in new ways. You can find a job in which you discover that you have more energy than you ever imagined. This is a gift, enjoy it.

The moral of our story is dream but execute. Persist, but know when to move on. Do not be a frog in a pot of water. Teams can work together beautifully. Expand your definition of success. Onward!

Second Contributor: Acquired Senior Vice President (ASVP)

I am often asked, if I had it to do all over again, whether I would have sold my consulting company to the Founder.

One surprising revelation from the entire experience of selling my company is that the lessons I learned are both professional as well as personal and it is very difficult for me to separate one from the other. You will find this evident throughout my portion of this chapter. Read on as I navigate through this mess called "life lessons."

Many of the lessons I learned were the result of having a non-compete clause with the Company that went into effect after I resigned. Having signed a non-compete clause meant that I could not approach the Company's clients, who were really originally my clients, for consulting work. The document I signed as a condition of the acquisition said, in effect, that I could "not compete" with the Company for consulting clients or assignments for six months if I resigned from the Company. I had put myself out of work. I was sidelined. It was maddening because many of my old clients called <u>me</u> and wanted me to work with them and I had to say "no." I was quiescently frozen.

I took these six, non-competing, months to reflect about what I wanted to do with the rest of my life. I spoke with my partner, family, friends, ex-employees, and even some old competitors. I tried to look at as many alternatives as possible. I received and turned down unsolicited job offers. What did I want to do? Did I want to remain an entrepreneur, begin and grow another consulting practice, train and manage new staff and shoulder the yoke of sales revenue generation or was there an alternative for me? Instead of this old and familiar path, I chose to become a one-man consultant working with a loose network of independent contractors in the same industry that I have been affiliated with for over twenty years. I have tried to select a life that gives me flexibility without the financial responsibility of employees. And so far, so good.

Okay, now I have a new professional direction and I have had some time off to reflect and get my energy back. I have played the video of my two-year, white-water trip over Niagara Falls with the Company in my head a hundred times, trying to see as clearly as possible what really happened and what I might have done differently. Here are my key lessons from my experience with the Company:

- **"Due Diligence" Is Not Just A Professional Term:** "Due Diligence" is one of those short-hand phrases that means different professional tasks from one industry to another, but its primary definition is that when an entity with fiduciary responsibility is acquiring anything substantial, such as my consulting practice or an office building or an apartment complex, on behalf of its stakeholders, the buyer has the responsibility to be duly diligent when examining the acquisition. I now know that due diligence is not just the job of the buyer but it is also the responsibility of the seller to examine the buyer. I now know that due diligence for me, the seller, was more complex than just asking the Company, the buyer, general questions about finances, relationships with key vendors and where my office will be located. I now know that professional due diligence must be accompanied by personal due diligence to ensure that there is an alignment of values and professional ethics between buyer and seller. In other words, date each other before getting married. Sounds like common sense but emotion is a powerful driver.

- In retrospect, even before I was approached by the Company, I wanted the responsibility of being the sole-proprietor for my moderately-sized consulting practice to be over. Though I enjoyed the work, I hated the pressure to constantly produce sales and to keep the revenue pipeline robust. I felt extremely responsible for the well-being of my employees but I disliked having to manage them. I felt a desire to mentor rather than to discipline. I naively (boy, I use that word a lot) thought that getting a business partner would allow me to get out from under the sales/management/owner burden. I couldn't have been more incorrect.

- Conducting due-diligence, in its simplest form for me should have been the process of gaining an understanding of the opportunities and risks associated with being acquired. Oh, I thought I completely understood the financial situation of the Company. I knew that the sales in their previous twelve months had been one-third that of my firm, but I allowed myself to believe that what the Founder and Chairman were telling me was true about their Company. Simply, I was in denial.

   There was another side to my due diligence to which I should have paid more attention – the personal side of due diligence. I should have asked more questions of the Founder that would have indicated whether we were a good emotional fit. Were our values similar? What responsibility did the Founder feel toward the Company's employees? Did the Founder genuinely work productively or were excuses such as, "I am exhausted. I stayed up until 2:00 am to put this contract together" constantly being floated when the contract could have taken the executive assistant 45 minutes to put together? Were the Founder's strengths in areas in which I was weak? Ah, which leads me to the next subject...

- **Understand Your Strengths and Know Your Weaknesses**: In business it is important to surround yourself with those who have strengths in areas in which you are weak. I luckily embraced this realistic approach early on when, as my business grew, I hired and promoted people whose abilities *complemented* mine. I knew I was good at sales but I had to admit that I was not as strong in the analytic aspects of our business as I wished to be. The folks I hired were strong analytically, and our team worked well together.

The Founder, in contrast, wanted to be surrounded only with those who wanted to be wildly successful...quickly! The Founder and the Chairman had disrespect for those employees who could do the actual work of the Company and get from A to B to C.

The problem with this thinking is that they did not realize that they needed employees who could systematically go from A to B to C. They unfortunately respected only those who talked a good game.

- **View Change as an Opportunity:** Well, this may not be an original idea but it can help you through some tough times. We all feel differently about change. Some of us thrive on change, others are immobile when faced with change.

  I was ecstatic at the opportunity I felt selling my firm to the Company presented. Not only could I get out of the burden of responsibility, as I have described it, but being acquired meant a physical household move from the Midwest to the West Coast. I viewed these changes as blessed events.

- **Experience Failure as an Opportunity to Conquer Your Fear of Failure:** I have always had a fear of failure. This fear has driven me to such an extent that I became obsessed with succeeding. When the merger with the Company failed, I was surprised when I was told by many well-meaning folks to see it not as a failure, but as a success, because I had sold my business. But I *knew* it was a failure. My worst fear was a reality.

So here I am. The acquisition I so wanted to succeed failed. I spent six months adrift and waiting for that horrible non-compete clause to expire; I was forced to do nothing. But strangely, the time for reflection became a time for renewal. I re-packaged my professional life to give myself flexibility and freedom. I succeeded in reducing what to me were tremendous professional responsibilities. I was honest enough and smart enough not to return to the familiar just because it was familiar. I discovered, and still believe, that I have many opportunities to explore, both professionally and personally.

Above all, I have learned that "failure" is a point in time, not a permanent condition. I have learned that I can recover from it. I won't go back to being the same person in the same place but I may be a better person in a new place and that is now OK with me. Should I ever again be confronted with my own failure, I will accept it, move on, and look for opportunities that change will provide.

Here are my Survival Tips when you find yourself on the Island of Regret:

- Take a deep breath and, you were probably afraid that I was going to say this, keep your sense of humor when everything is falling down around you. Sorry, but there it is. It is true that a good laugh allows you to see that you will not always be starving and thirsty in your current dark, scorpion-filled, airless, self-inflicted pit.

- Take strength from the fact that you experienced your worst fear and did not run screaming off a cliff. You have given yourself a second chance.

- Take courage that you went after your dream – most people never even try.

- Take pride that failure forced your employees to take up new professional challenges and that your employees were all so talented that, without exception, they have moved on to better themselves.

- Take comfort – you are not the only person on the face of this planet with worthless stock!

If I had it to do all over again, would I sell my consulting company to the Founder? I don't know the answer to that, but at least know that I now have the skills to deal with the outcome.

What ever happened to the Contributors?
Here is our Epilogue

VP & ASVP: The Vice President and the Acquired Senior Vice President managed and organized the writing of this book. She is a consultant when she discovers an interesting assignment and the ASVP started his own small, profitable consulting practice. No, he does not want to sell his consulting business!

Jill-Of-All-Trades: Hope sprang eternal for Jill and she joined another high-tech start-up company. This time, she found a company that was well funded and whose founder was focused on success. Jill now has stock options worth a lot of money. Go, Jill!

High School Intern: Our Intern became a brilliant undergraduate student at the University of California-Berkeley.

Second Receptionist: Our Receptionist was in the sequel to the movie The Hulk and has been successful in regional Shakespeare plays. Break a leg!

CTO2: Our Chief Technology Officer 2 is now a consultant six months of the year and sails the crystal waters of the South Seas the other six months of the year. Really.

Director of Quantitative Data: Our DQD is President of a real estate development company and no longer stirring the "secret sauce."

Customer Service Representative: Our CSR found a job three days after being laid off from the Company. He earns a ton of money working in the home re-finance business and has achieved his goal of purchasing his own residential loft.

Salesman #1: Our original, lonely salesman went to work for a large, national, consulting company and doubled his salary.

Executive Vice President of Sales and Marketing: The EVP splits his time between wilderness biking and foreign travel. Retirement is not that bad, after all!

Director of Sales: Needing to apply himself to something other than sales, the Director of Sales sadly abandoned the Pacific Ocean surf and returned to the Midwest where he opened his own web-design business.

Marketing Maven: Maven joined a company where she supervises thirteen people and has control over the marketing message and the marketing process.

Accountant of the Acquired Consulting Firm: Our accountant is now an office manager for a law firm and has increased her salary and her authority.

Senior Consultant for Professional Services: Our Senior Consultant is happily working as a free-lance consultant and has increased his salary by 50%.

Saintly Operations Manager: Our SOM is now working for the public sector, (see, we told you she is a saint), and is loved by all who come into contact with her.

The Founder's Final Executive Assistant: The FEA has moved to Las Vegas because it is the only world stranger than that of the Company and has a job she loves working out of her home.

Part-time Bookkeeper: The PTB currently works, part-time, for a non-profit organization. Peace and love.

The Spouse of the VP: The Spouse is still managing his own firm successfully. He completely supported the VP in her effort to get this book published and he is happy to report that dinner is much less stressful now!

We have all moved on and quite successfully!

Our Annotated Bibliography

Books on Business and Leadership: We have culled through our shelves and here are the books we recommend on a variety of business topics. These may not be the newest books on each topic but we have found them all to be honest, useful and memorable:

Geoffrey Moore's *Crossing the Chasm* is a wonderful book that details how to sell high-tech products to mainstream customers. CTO2 and the VP both read this classic book and they wished the Founder and the Chairman had as well. Read or re-read it – it is a treasure!

The best book on how to think about technology when you are developing an innovative product for the first time is Donald Norman's truthful, insightful book, *The Invisible Computer: Why Good Products Can Fail, The Personal Computer Is So Complex, and Information Appliances are The Solution.* At least read Chapters One and Four!

An excellent book that addresses where your company is in its lifecycle and describes the tools for predicting and analyzing organizational behavior as well as changing it is Ichak Adizes *Corporate Lifecycles – How and Why Corporations Grow and Die and What to Do About It.*

No one can teach the entrepreneur more about the disciplines, yes, **disciplines**, that are needed to be successful than

Michael Gerber. We recommend *E-Myth Mastery: Seven Essential Disciplines for Building a World Class Business* and *The E-Myth Revisited: Why Most Small Businesses Don't Work and What to Do About It* to all entrepreneurs. Oh, heck, we recommend all of Michael Gerber's books.

When you work for an Extreme Boss, and the probability is good that one day you will, please read *Working with You is Killing Me.* Extreme Bosses are described on page 128 and The Controlling Egomaniac is described on Page 141. Katherine Crowley and Kathi Elster describe our Founder perfectly and if we had had this resource we would have had a better understanding of the bizarre behavior that we witnessed.

Michael Feiner's book, *The Feiner Points of Leadership,* won us over right from the Introduction in which he says that in too many companies, "Results don't reflect the collective effort of the employees." Well, we were living proof of that. We also agree with him when he says that good managers generate order, consistency, and predictability. What a positive contrast that vision is to the chaos we had to deal with!

Warren Bennis hits a major chord with us when he discusses "innovative learning" in his classic book, *On Becoming A Leader.* He argues, and we heartedly agree, that company leaders can learn by simply listening to others, which, for our Founder, was not simple at all. Leaders who listen and learn from others create a business environment, according to Dr. Bennis, in which employees express themselves rather than just explain themselves. Imagine how things might have turned out differently for us had we worked in this sort of free-exchange environment! Get a copy of *On Becoming A Leader* and listen and learn!

James Kouzes and Barry Posner have written *The Leadership Challenge,* which is an acknowledged classic on business leadership and clearly identifies five practices of exemplary, personal-best, leadership. Clearly, we experienced none of the five practices but the one that stood out to us, because it was unusual, was Number Five: Encourage the Heart, and we read their book *Encourage the Heart* to learn more. We recommend that you do, too. And, just to pour salt in our wounds, we also read *Resonant Leadership*, by Richard Boyatzis and Annie McKee. Very truthfully, we wept our way through *Resonant Leadership.* The Boyatzis/McKee wondrous vision of the positive, productive job environment that is a result of managers who espouse optimism and hope in their employees was what we thought we could create when we joined the Company. Oh, well. Buy tissue when you buy the book.

Daniel Goleman's *Working with Emotional Intelligence* is our favorite book on the topic. Take it out and re-read the whole book.

It may be time to review a couple of the most important lessons from Dr. Richard Carlson's book, *Don't Sweat the Small Stuff at Work.* May we suggest starting on Page 44 for his essay on acknowledging others and then, perhaps, re-reading Chapter 49, Page 140, where we are reminded to see people as people rather than as chess pieces.

Marilyn Haight's book, *Who's Afraid of The Big, Bad Boss*, identifies thirteen types of bad bosses. The unique part of this book is that she gives the employee tips on how to identify these bad bosses by what they say in the job interview so that they can be avoided. Haight also offers up some tough love and tells you when you should just start looking for another job. We all wish her advice had been available to us...

Patrick Lencioni does more than just discuss a similar, hopeless morass in *The Five Dysfunctions of a Team*. On Page 194 of his book, he identifies those five dysfunctions and, beginning on Page 195, he actually gives you his methods of overcoming them. Get a copy of his book!

Before you take on the assignment of developing software on an unrealistically low budget and with an unrealistically short deadline, you might want to read *Death March: The Complete Software Developer's Guide to Surviving "Mission Impossible" Projects* by Edward Yourdon. Misery loves company.

The second edition of *The Strategy and Tactics of Pricing* by Thomas Nagle and Reed Holden has an excellent discussion that starts on Page 168 on how to price an innovative product. Yes, the rest of the book is good but if you have to price an innovative product, start on Page 168.

The Thin Book of Appreciative Inquiry by Sue Annis Hammond is a great book to read when deciding what kind of off-site, senior management meeting you should hold next.

Michael Maccoby's book, *The Productive Narcissist*, provides a direct and clear picture of the better side of working with the narcissist. Our narcissist was more Perilous than Productive, but you may be luckier. If you are not, a blunt, eye-opening, book that we hope you will never have to read, but just in case you do, is Eleanor Payson's *The Wizard of Oz and Other Narcissists.* Want even more information on the N word? Sandy Hotchkiss, author of *Why is it Always About You,* spells out the seven narcissistic deadly sins. You will not be able to live in denial after reading her book.

And, of course, on many occasions we thought a spy from *Dilbert* was in our office as many of the wacky things in the comic strip were close to our daily experience. We find *Dilbert* is a good reality check. When your job approaches *Dilbertonian* levels, get your resume ready!

Books on Writing Books: None of us had ever been published in other than trade magazines before this book. Should you ever decide to write a book, here are the books we found most useful and helpful:

Ann Lamott's *Bird by Bird* is the best book ever written about the writing experience. If you find yourself worrying about your brain tumor every time you sit down in front of your computer, read this great book, and heal yourself.

Thinking Like Your Editor by Susan Rabiner is a great place to learn how editors think, (and it's not like we think), and how to write a book proposal.

The Self-Publishing Manual: How to Write, Print and Sell Your Own Book by Dan Poynter is a great source of publishing industry information even if you do not self-publish. *Guerrilla Marketing for Writers* by Levinson, Frishman, and Larsen is our marketing bible.

Jeff Herman's *Guide to Book Publishers, Editors, and Literary Agents* is indispensable and actually fun to read.

As for the writing itself, we found inspiration in *Sin & Syntax*, by Constance Hale. How did she write a grammar book that reads like a novel? If you didn't like our interjections (sheesh, lordy, and dammit), you have *Sin & Syntax* to blame. Also, we found the discussion of what "is" is, pages 63 and 64, tremendously useful. We edited fifty-three "is's" out of our book and should have gone for more.

A second inspiration on the writing itself was William Zinsser's classic, *On Writing Well*. We found his discussion of The Audience, Chapter Five, reassuring because we had been told to picture our readers and we couldn't. We hoped for lots of readers who all looked different and we had been advised that this was the road to disaster. Chapter Five set us straight. The

Memoir, Chapter Fourteen, gave us permission to write each chapter as the individuals we were when we worked for the Company rather than produce twenty-one homogenized chapters.

We didn't even think of skipping these great tools:

- a good dictionary,
- *The Elements of Style* by Strunk and White, and,
- *The Elements of Grammar* by Margaret Shertzer.

Even with these wonderful guides it can be hard to get everything right.

And best of luck from us to you!

Acknowledgements

Thanks to my supportive family members:

My Spouse, who wrote, edited, encouraged me, nagged me,

and made the cover a reality,

My Mother, who edited and encouraged me,

My Father, who edited and encouraged me,

My Sister-in-law, JHH, who read, remembered, and

provided an opportunity for me.

Thanks to my supportive co-workers who also walked this

walk with me:

JG, who wrote and read,

RB, who read, and suggested that a Narrator wouldn't hurt.

Thanks to supportive friends, in alphabetical order:

CC, who read, commented, and encouraged me,

LG, who read, commented, encouraged, and said, "The bird

stays on the cover"

BG who enabled me to get into the weeds of publishing,

S. O'K, who read and encouraged me.

About the Editor

The editor of this book is a business consultant who has taught business management students at the college and university level on both the east and west coasts. The editor has an MBA, with honors, from Boston University.